LATER
LIFE
FAMILIES

FAMILY STUDIES TEXT SERIES

Series Editor: RICHARD J. GELLES, *University of Rhode Island*
Series Associate Editor: ALEXA A. ALBERT, *University of Rhode Island*

This series of textbooks is designed to examine topics relevant to a broad view of family studies. The series is aimed primarily at undergraduate students of family sociology and family relations, among others. Individual volumes will be useful to students in psychology, home economics, counseling, human services, social work and other related fields. Core texts in the series cover such subjects as theory and conceptual design, research methods, family history, cross-cultural perspectives, and life course analysis. Other texts will cover traditional topics, such as dating and mate selection, parenthood, divorce and remarriage, and family power. Topics that have been receiving more recent public attention will also be dealt with, including family violence, later life families, and fatherhood.

Because of their wide range and coverage, Family Studies Texts can be used singly or collectively to supplement a standard text or to replace one. These books will be of interest to both students and professionals in a variety of disciplines.

Volumes in this series:

1. LATER LIFE FAMILIES
   Timothy H. Brubaker

2. INTIMATE VIOLENCE IN FAMILIES
   Richard J. Gelles & Claire Pedrick Cornell

Volumes planned for this series:

THEORIES OF FAMILY LIFE, David M. Klein

THE PATHS OF MARRIAGE, Bernard Murstein

FAMILY RESEARCH METHODS, Brent C. Miller

WORK AND FAMILY LIFE, Patricia Voydanoff

FAMILY POWER, Maximiliane Szinovacz

BECOMING A PARENT, Ralph LaRossa

FAMILY STRESS, Pauline Boss

DIVORCE, Sharon J. Price & Patrick McHenry

REMARRIAGE, Marilyn Ihinger-Tallman & Kay Pasley

CONCEPTUAL FRAMEWORKS FOR FAMILY STUDIES,
   Keith Farrington

LATER
LIFE
FAMILIES

Timothy H. Brubaker

FAMILY STUDIES
TEXT SERIES 1

SAGE PUBLICATIONS
Beverly Hills   London   New Delhi

*This book is dedicated to those with
whom I hope to enjoy later life—
Ellie, Laurie Cate, Christie Beth,
and Puffin.*

Copyright © 1985 by Sage Publications, Inc.

For information address:

SAGE Publications, Inc.
275 South Beverly Drive
Beverly Hills, California 90212

SAGE Publications India Pvt. Ltd.
C-236 Defence Colony
New Delhi 110 024, India

SAGE Publications Ltd
28 Banner Street
London EC1Y 8QE, England

Printed in the United States of America

Library of Congress Cataloging in Publication Data

Brubaker, Timothy H.
  Later life families.

  (Family studies text series ; v. 1)
  Bibliography: p.
  Includes index.
  1. Aged—United States—Family relationships.
2. Aged—United States—Social conditions. 3. Family—
United States—Social conditions. I. Title. II. Series.
HQ1064.U5B77   1984   306.8'7   84-18065
ISBN 0-8039-2293-0
ISBN 0-8039-2294-9 (pbk.)

FIRST PRINTING

Contents

Preface

THIS BOOK IS BASED ON THE PREMISE that later life families provide an intriguing look at human relationships. They are relationships that have a
long history of interaction, and their coping strategies have been tested.
Recognition that continuity permeates many of these relationships will
either encourage us to renegotiate our family bonds or be thankful that
we have strong family relationships.

Attention has been directed toward later life families because the
topic had not received a great deal of attention until the mid-1970s. As
gerontological course offerings expanded, the limited amount of
research on this topic became more apparent. Concomitantly, research
money became available to study later life family relationships. The
result is an increased number of studies focusing on later life families.

The primary objective of this book is to review studies on later life
family patterns. Gerontologists have frequently stated that the later life
family is alive and well. This book examines the research that supports
this contention. Later life families involve vibrant responsive social
relationships that deal with changes associated with aging. Generally,
aging family members are not ignored by the younger generations. At
the same time, there are aspects of these relationships that need
support and assistance. This book identifies some of these aspects and
suggests futures changes relevant to later life families.

Within the past twenty years family sociologists and gerontologists
have focused their attention on the study of family relationships during
the later stages of the family life cycle. Research during the 1960s was
reviewed in Lillian Troll's article published in the *Journal of Marriage
and Family Relations* in 1971. During the 1970s, research on this topic
began to multiply and several reviews were published. Troll expanded
her article into a book and published *Families in Later Life* with Sheila
Miller and Robert C. Atchley in 1979. Gordon Streib and Ruth Beck
summarized the research on later life families during the 1970s in the
Journal of Marriage and the Family in 1981. Also, during this time, two
special issues of *The Family Coordinator* were devoted to aging families. The first was published in 1972 and edited by Felix Berardo, and the
second in 1978 was co-edited by Timothy H. Brubaker and Lawrence E.
Sneden. The early 1980s has evidenced a flurry of publications on this
topic. This book seeks to integrate the most recent research with
previous findings.

Acknowledgments

ANY BOOK IS THE FRUIT of many people, and this book is no exception. My perspective on later life family relationships has been influenced by mentors and colleagues from Iowa State University and the Midwest Council for Social Research on Aging. Their tutelage and stimulating critical thought continue to underpin my professional orientation. I am grateful for these professional relationships.

This book would not have been initiated without the urging of the editors at Sage Publications, whose willingness to prod and support me during this project is appreciated.

Rich Gelles, editor of this series, is recognized for his prompt critiques and encouragement at each stage of this project. Also, Lynn Vesey is thanked for her library searches. Gratitude is expressed to Sarah Seals, Carol Webb, and Crystal Davis for help in the creation of the index. These persons made this tedious task enjoyable most of the time.

Special thanks is given to Ellie Brubaker, who is my wife, colleague, and critic. I appreciated her support and willingness to critique each chapter of this book. Without her, this book would never have been completed.

Appreciation is given to the Family and Child Studies Center and the Department of Home Economics and Consumer Sciences of Miami University. A university-assigned research appointment provided the time to devote to this project.

It is the above crew who helped sail this ship into port on schedule. To each, I am grateful.

CHAPTER
1

Later Life Families

Family 1: Irene and Matt are both 75 years old and have been married for 52 years. Matt retired from teaching high school ten years ago and was very active until last year, when he became ill and was hospitalized twice. Following his return home from the hospital, Irene cared for him. Irene has been a housewife throughout their marriage. Both are satisfied with their marriage and claim that it has gotten better since the children left home and Matt retired. They now have more time to focus on each other. Their two children are married and their daughter lives about ten minutes from their house. Their son lives in a town about thirty miles away. Irene and Matt enjoy their four grandchildren and two great-grandchildren whom they see quite often.

Family 2: Sam and Martha have been married two years. Sam is 68 years old and Martha is 56 years old. Both had been widowed (Sam for eleven months and Martha for two years) and had known each other for many years before either of their spouses passed away. Their marriage is satisfying. Sam has three children and seven grandchildren. One son lives close by, but his other son and daughter live three hours from him. Martha's daughter lives next door and she visits with her two grandchildren every day. Sam is retired from the telephone company, and Martha continues to work full time at the local library.

Family 3: Judith, 43, has been divorced for fifteen years and her daughter, 23, married last year after graduating from college. Judith's son, 25, has been married for five years and has two children. Judith visits her son two or three times a week and spends a great deal of time with her grandchildren. She works at a local hospital as a nurse's aide and is very happy with her job. She hopes to remarry sometime, but she is not seeing anyone at the present time.

Family 4: Josephine, 84, has been widowed for fifteen years and lives in an affluent retirement community where she has organized a sewing circle. Josephine taught high school home economics for forty-five years before she retired twenty years ago. She now uses her teaching skills to teach other people how to sew. Her son sees her twice a month, and about once a month her granddaughter brings her first great-grandson to visit. Her daughter lives 500 miles away and writes or telephones often but seldom visits. She infrequently sees her daughter's children and their families. Josephine is very fond of her former husband and has not wanted to remarry. Although she is having some problems getting around, she expects these difficulties because she is "old."

What do all these families have in common? They all include persons who have been married at some time within their lives and all have children. All have grandchildren and some have great-grandchildren. One family has been married more than fifty years, another for only two years. One family divorced many years ago, and one wife was widowed fifteen years ago. Some have retired and others are working full-time. The ages vary from 43 to 84 years. Since these families represent later life families, what is the common denominator between the families?

The definition and characteristics of later life families will be discussed in this chapter. It is important to remember that there are differences and similarities between them.

DEFINITION OF LATER LIFE FAMILIES

Family scholars have directed their attention to the study of the family over the life cycle. The family life cycle refers to "a predictability about family development that helps us know what to expect of any given family at any given stage" (Duvall, 1977: 141). The family life cycle approach is "based on the recognition of successive phases and patterns as they occur within the continuity of family living over the years" (p. 141). Generally, this approach to the study of the family begins with the establishment of a couple's relationship through marriage and focuses on the addition of the couple's children. The couple progresses through the stages of the family life cycle as the children mature and eventually initiate their own marital relationships. Consequently, many family scholars have directed their research to the early stages of the family life cycle.

The primary focus of this book is on families who have progressed to the later stages of the family life cycle and are dealing with the tasks associated with later life. Specifically, *"later life families" refers to families who are beyond the child-rearing years and have begun to launch their children* (Brubaker, 1983). At this time in the family life cycle, the nuclear unit is contracting rather than expanding (Duvall, 1977). The emphasis is on the *remaining members* of the family of orientation *after* the children have initiated their own families of procreation. As illustrated in the above cases the remaining members may include a husband and wife who have been married for many years. Or, one spouse may be the primary survivor in the family of orientation because he or she divorced or became widowed. The survivor may remarry, and the later life family may include persons who were previously not part of the family. The remarriage may combine two families of orientation in the later years.

The use of chronological age to distinguish later life families from young or middle life families is problematic (Troll et al., 1979). Since couples marry and have children at different ages, they launch their children at different ages. Consequently, a person may be 55 years of age and still have children living at home. Or, similar to Judith in family 3, another individual aged 45 years may have two adult children who have begun their own families of procreation. When children leave home, the remaining person(s) need(s) to address issues related to family life regardless of age. Thus, chronological age alone is not an appropriate indicator of later life families.

Since children leaving their families of orientation is used as the primary requisite for defining later life families, a problem occurs with the small number of couples who have no children. When do childless couples become later life families? The family life cycle approach to the study of the family has difficulty dealing with these couples. Generally, childless couples are considered to be in the later life stages if either of the members is aged 50 years or above. Most people follow similar life courses (Atchley, 1980; Neugarten et al., 1965); for example, there seems to be a range of years during which most individuals marry, have children, establish a career, and retire. Atchley (1976) suggested that age 50 may be a reasonable estimate of the chronological age by which most individuals experience the tasks typically associated with later life. Therefore, recognizing the problems with chronological age and not having a better indicator, the age of 50 will be used as crude indicator of later life families for the few couples who do not have offspring.

THE LATER STAGES

Evelyn Duvall (1977) identified eight stages of the family life cycle demarcated by the maturation of offspring within the nuclear family. The stages included the *married couple, childbearing, preschool-age, school age, teenage, launching center, middled-aged parents,* and *aging family members.* The last two stages—middle-aged parent (empty nest to retirement) and the aging family (retirement to death of both spouses)—are related to later life families. Table 1.1 identifies a number of tasks belonging to these two stages that later life families address.

In the middle-aged stage, the tasks related to the children leaving home and the reorganization of the family around the remaining

TABLE 1.1
Developmental Tasks of Later Life Family

Middle-Aged (empty nest to retirement)
  (1) providing for comfortable, healthful well-being
  (2) allocating resources for present and future needs
  (3) developing patterns of complementarity
  (4) undertaking appropriate social roles
  (5) assuming marital satisfaction
  (6) enlarging the family circle
  (7) participating in life beyond the home
  (8) affirming life's control values

Aging Couple (retirement to death of a spouse)
  (1) making satisfying living arrangements as aging progresses
  (2) adjusting to retirement income
  (3) establishing comfortable routines
  (4) safeguarding physical and mental health
  (5) maintaining love, sex, and marital relations
  (6) remaining in touch with other family members
  (7) keeping active and involved
  (8) finding meaning in life

Adapted from Duvall (1977: 365, 390).

members. In this book, primary concern is with the latter activities. Many later life families enter an "empty nest" period in which they adjust their lifestyles around the husband and wife roles. Parental tasks are redefined because the children are no longer living at home and most have initiated their own families of procreation. For some couples, this is the first time in twenty to thirty years that they have been living together without children in the household. Household activities may be reallocated. Couples have more opportunity to enhance positive or exacerbate problematic aspects of their relationships. Men and women who have careers are approaching their peaks—their job-related responsibilities may be demanding and their incomes may be the highest they have ever experienced.

At the same time, many couples approach or consider retirement. With the children gone, some wives begin or reenter a career, and the couple has another new encounter to which they must adjust. Thus the empty nest period is the initial contraction phase, and later life families must deal with issues related to the movement of children out of the household. While the reduction in the size of the household is the primary focus, empty nest couples are also interested in the addition of new members to the family through marriage and birth. Dealing with in-laws and becoming grandparents are expansion issues of concern to later life couples.

The aging family further contracts in a number of ways. First, it is marked by retirement—Duvall (1977) suggested that the final stage in the family life cycle is begun with retirement. Working members of the marital unit need to develop lifestyles that are not centered on or do not include the jobs they held for many years. Some may retire from full-time employment and accept part-time work. Others may retire from one job and take another. Many retire, become involved in other activities, and are not employed at all. In any case, the family—spouse and children—responds to the retiree's new way of life. This event may create an opportunity for couples to spend more time together and further strengthen their marital relationships—or it may further illumi- nate the shadowy aspects of a marriage.

The aging family will also need to address the aging process and any health problems that may develop. As marital partners age and their health becomes problematic, the healthier spouse may become the caregiver for the less healthy person. Care may be provided in the home, or in an institution such as a nursing home; most of the care is within the home. Some couples may move to a retirement community in which care is provided. Eventually, the aging couple will need to deal with the death of one spouse. The survivor's tasks include adjustment to additional contraction of the family unit as well as maintenance of family relationships with children and grandchildren. If the survivor remarries, the task of continuing the family relationships may be compounded.

CHANGING FAMILY LIFE CYCLE

In comparing the demographics of the family from early 1900 to the 1970, demographer Paul Glick of the U.S. Bureau of the Census (1977) concluded that because of the longer life span and other changes in the family and society, the empty nest period has increased from two to thirteen years. With the longer empty nest period, *many families spent four to five times more years as a couple in the later stages than in the early stages of the family life cycle.* Changes in the timing of the birth of the first child are also important to the family life cycle. Glick (1977) noted that the birth rate has decreased so that there are fewer children within a family. Today, the average family has one or two children instead of three or four as in the mid 1950s. Since the number of children is smaller and persons live longer, fewer years are devoted to childrearing. Consequently, the number of years spent in the empty nest period is increased. Although much family research has focused on the early phases of marriage, it is clear that families live many years in the later stages of the family life cycle.

The timing of marriage and the birth of the first child have interesting implications for later life families. Individuals who postpone the birth of the first child may preclude the possibility of having five- or six-generation families. For example, if a woman has a child at age 18, and each subsequent generation has its first child at 18, the family could include six generations if the first woman lived to be 74. However, if the same woman postponed the birth of her first child until age 30, and subsequent generations did likewise, the family could be no larger than three or four generations. Thus, the family network would be approximately twice as large for the woman who had her first child at a younger age.

UNIQUE ASPECTS OF LATER LIFE FAMILIES

There are two unique aspects of later life families that are important to the study of these families. The first, as noted above, is that most later life families are multigenerational. When several generations exist within the family, the oldest persons may not be the only later life couples in the family network. In some family systems, the oldest members are providing care to less healthy, younger persons. The multigenerational aspect and potential for more than two generations are important factors to consider when examining the major life events (retirement, death of a spouse) and health status of later life couples.

Another unique aspect is the lengthy family history (Brubaker, 1983). Later life families have been interacting, coping, making decisions, and developing affection and hostilities for many years. *When a couple launches a child and addresses the tasks associated with the middle and later years, they have a family track record on which to interact.* Unlike recently married couples, older couples have experienced many events together, and they may be able to predict the other's behavior with some degree of accuracy. This history may contribute positively or negatively to the family. For example, marital satisfaction may be enhanced because a satisfied couple can spend more time together while an unsatisfied couple becomes less satisfied. A strong parent-child relationship may be strengthened while a weak one may deteriorate further. Since a later life family is either blessed or haunted by its family history, it is crucial for family researchers and practitioners to become familiar with the previous family interactions to understand fully later life family interactions. The continuity of family behavior cannot be underestimated.

Before research on later life families is reviewed, demographics for these families are presented. Since census data are categorized by age and not stage in the family life cycle, the demographics are presented for persons 45 years and above in most instances.

MARITAL STATUS OF THE ELDERLY

Statistics on the marital status of older persons indicate that men are usually married and women are likely to married and widowed (see Table 1.2). While the majority of older men are married, the proportion declines somewhat as men reach ages 75 years and over. Women under age 65 years, however, are most likely to be married and those 65 years and older are likely to be widowed. For example, two-thirds of the women aged 55 to 64 years are married, and slightly more than two-thirds aged 75 years and over are widowed. In the oldest age category, slightly more than one out of five women are married.

As might be expected, the portion of widowers increases with age. There are approximately four times as many widowers aged 75 years and over than widowers aged 55 to 64 years. Divorced and never-married persons account for a small proportion of the elderly. With the exception of the never-married women, the numbers and percentages of divorced and never-married persons decline with age. The proportion of never-married women appear to increase slightly with age.

It is no surprise that most older men live with their spouses and many older women live alone or with a nonrelative (Brubaker, 1983; Brotman, 1981). Specifically, 52 percent of women 75 years and older live alone or with a nonrelative and 68 percent of men the same age live with a spouse. Less than one-quarter of the women aged 75 years and above live with a spouse. For women aged 65 to 74 years, less than one-half live with a spouse and nearly 40 percent live alone or with a nonrelative.

TABLE 1.2
Marital Status of Men and Women Aged 55 Years and Over
(March 1982)[a]

	Male		Female	
	Number[b]	%	Number	%
Aged 55-64 years				
married, spouse present	8,520	83.5	7,907	67.7
married, spouse absent	299	2.9	364	3.1
widowed	355	3.5	2,019	17.3
divorced	553	5.4	898	7.7
never married	472	4.6	484	4.2
Aged 65-74 years				
married, spouse present	5,520	81.5	4,400	49.3
married, spouse absent	166	2.5	180	2.0
widowed	510	7.5	3,419	38.3
divorced	244	3.6	458	5.1
never married	331	4.9	469	5.3
Aged 75 years and over				
married, spouse present	2,484	70.2	1,343	22.4
married, spouse absent	82	2.3	771	1.2
widowed	770	21.7	4,104	68.5
divorced	86	2.4	110	1.8
never married	118	3.3	365	6.1

SOURCE: U.S. Department of Commerce (1983: 8).
a. All races.
b. Number in thousands.

Women, more than men, are likely to live with another relative (many times an adult child).

In summary, marriage is a lifestyle experienced by most older people. These data suggest that the elderly population is either married or has been married. Most likely, older men are married and living with their wives while older women are widowed and living alone or with a nonrelative. Compared to older men, older women more often live with another relative.

THE NEVER MARRIEDS

The proportion of older bachelors and unmarried women has declined over the past twelve years (see Table 1.3). The Bureau of the

TABLE 1.3
Percentage of Never-Married Men and Women Aged 45 Years and Over:
1982, 1980, 1970

	Women			Men		
	1982	1980	1970	1982	1980	1970
45-54 years	4.1	4.7	4.9	5.4	6.1	7.5
55-64 years	4.1	4.5	6.8	4.6	5.3	7.8
65 years and over	5.6	5.9	7.7	4.4	4.9	7.5

SOURCE: U.S. Department of Commerce (1983: 2).

Census (U.S. Department of Commerce, 1983) reported that 7.5 percent of men aged 65 years and above had never married in 1970, while in
1982, 4.4 percent had not married. A similar decline is evidenced for
women aged 65 years and older. In fact, there was a 41 percent decline
in the proportion of older, never-married men from 1970 to 1982 and a
27 percent decline for never-married women. For women aged 55 to 64
years, there was a 40 percent decline, and for men, a 41 percent decline
in the proportion of never marrieds. These data suggest that never-
married older persons are a small segment of the elderly population and
the size of this group is decreasing. Marriage is an event experienced by
an increasing portion of older men and women.

ELDERLY DIVORCE

Similar to the number of younger persons who divorce, approximately twice as many older people are divorced in the 1980s than in the
1960s (U.S. Department of Commerce, 1983). For example, there were
53 divorced women aged 45 to 64 years for every 1000 married women
in 1960. In 1982, there were 129 divorcees for every 1000 married
women in the same age group. For women aged 65 years and above,
there were 44 per 1000 in 1960 and 99 per 1000 in 1982. Divorces for
older men also increased. In 1960, there were 39 divorced men aged 45
to 64 years per 1000 married men, while in 1982 there were 83. Men
aged 65 years and above had 24 divorces per 1000 marriages in 1960 and
41 per 1000 marriages in 1982. The number of older persons who are
divorced has increased, and in addition, there are many older men and
women who have experienced divorce within their lifetimes. It should
be noted that these data do not distinguish between elderly who have

TABLE 1.4

Percentage of Divorces and Annulments by Age
(45 Years and Older) of Husband and Wife
at Time of Marriage and Decree: 1971, 1976, 1981

	1981	*1976*	*1971*
Age at time of marriage			
Husband			
45 years and over	4.5	4.8	5.0
Wife			
45 years and over	2.7	3.1	3.4
Age at time of decree			
Husband			
45-49 years	6.6	7.2	8.4
50-55 years	4.5	4.9	5.5
55-59 years	2.7	2.9	3.2
60-64 years	1.5	1.5	1.7
65 years and over	1.4	1.5	1.6
Wife			
45-49 years	4.8	5.6	6.8
50-54 years	3.0	3.5	4.0
55-59 years	1.8	1.9	2.0
60-64 years	.9	.9	.9
65 years and over	.8	.8	.8

SOURCE: U.S. Department of Health and Human Services (1984: 11, 12).

been divorced earlier in life and those who become divorced in the later years. There appears to be a slight decline in the percentages of older men and women who marry and later divorce. Table 1.4 presents the percentage of divorces by age of marriage and age at divorce decree. From 1971 to 1981, the percentage of men and women aged 65 years who married and later divorced declined slightly. The older the husband and wife, the less likely they are to divorce. For instance, men and women aged 45 to 49 years are approximately six times more likely to get divorced than persons aged 65 and above.

Becoming and being divorced in later life are significant processes of family life for some older persons. While some of divorced older persons remarry, many remain unmarried. Older divorced women are particularly disadvantaged in finding a marital partner. A potential research area concerns the differences between older persons who divorce in later life compared to those who divorce earlier in life and do not remarry. Do long-term divorced elderly differ from persons who divorced in later life?

TABLE 1.5

Number of Marriages, Marriage Rates by Previous Marital Status
for Men and Women Aged 65 Years and Over:
1970 and 1980[a]

| | Women | | | | Men | | | |
| | 1980 | | 1970 | | 1980 | | 1970 | |
	Number	Rate	Number	Rate	Number	Rate	Number	Rate
All marriages	18,431	2.2	15,011	2.4	33,286	15.2	31,032	15.6
First marriages	823	0.9	950	1.1	1,507	2.9	1,852	3.4
Remarriages[c]	17,260	2.3	13,951	2.5	31,280	19.0	28,968	19.9
previously widowed	12,673	2.1	10,588	2.3	20,992	17.8	21,436	19.4
previously divorced	2,505	5.3	1,658	6.1	6,539	22.8	4,292	23.6

SOURCE: National Center for Health Statistics (1983: 7).
a. Based on sample data.
b. Per 1000 population in specified group.
c. Excludes data from District of Columbia, Michigan, and Ohio in 1970, and Michigan, Ohio, and South Carolina in 1980.

REMARRIAGE IN LATER LIFE

The number of older people who marry for the first time or remarry is relatively small. Only 1 percent of all brides and 2 percent of all grooms were 65 years or older in 1975 (Glick, 1979). The marriage rates per 1000 eligible persons are low because out of this 1000, there are large numbers of men and women aged 65 years and over. Glick (1979) calculates the remarriage rates for older persons as 20 per 1000 for widowers and 2 per 1000 for widows. Divorced older men remarry at a rate of 31 per 1000, while divorced women remarry at a rate of 9 per 1000. Another study (Treas and VanHilst, 1976) concluded that marriage is for the young, and older people who marry are atypical. Clearly, marriage in later life is not a frequent event.

Is it more likely that never-married, divorced, or widowed older persons will marry? Similar to other ages, divorced older persons are more likely to marry than widowed. Bachelors and unmarried women are the least likely to marry (Table 1.5).

An analysis of remarriage statistics (Hacker, 1983) suggested that nearly 75 percent of divorced men aged 65 and over remarry while approximately 25 percent of their female counterparts remarry. Regardless of previous marital status, those who marry are most likely to marry widowed persons (Treas and VanHilst, 1976). Cleveland and Gianturco (1976) analyzed remarriage probabilities of widowed persons and illustrated that widowers are more likely to remarry than widows. Although the probabilities for remarriage decrease with age for both men and women, substantial fractions of older widowers remarry while very few older widows do so. Above age 75, 4 percent of the widowers in their sample remarried and the number of remarriages for widows was negligible. The median remarriage interval for widowers aged 65 to 74 years was 1.5 years and 1.3 years for those aged 75 years and above. For widows aged 65 to 74, the median interval is 3.8 years. Comparison of these data with rates for Black widowed men and women indicates that remarriage probabilities are lower and the interval before remarriage is greater for older Blacks.

As found in other age categories, men tend to marry younger women. Six out of ten divorced men remarry younger women while two out of ten divorced women marry younger men. One-third of the women remarry older men. This trend is supported by the social expectation that men should be older than their wives.

Differences in the male and female remarriage rates are related to the fewer number of available men and the tendency for men to marry younger women. Consequently, there are substantial numbers of older women who are divorced or widowed and who have few potential marriage partners. Since the 75 years and over category is growing, this situation will not change. Women aged 75 years and older will most likely be widowed and their probability of remarrying is low.

COHABITATION IN LATER LIFE

Within the past several years, many adults have decided to live together and not marry. The U.S. Census data indicate that the number of unmarried households has tripled in the past twelve years (U.S. Department of Commerce, 1983). Family scholars have used the term "cohabitation" to refer to these unmarried households. Although the U.S. Census definition of "unmarried household" may include individuals who are not living together "as man and wife," it is a crude indication of the number of unmarried persons who are cohabitating.

What proportion of the cohabitating households include older people? According to the U.S. Census, the proportion of cohabitating older persons has *decreased* by more than half since 1970 (see Table 1.6).

In 1970, approximately 22 percent of the cohabitating households included persons aged 65 years and over, whereas in 1982, this proportion was 5.5 percent. A decrease, though not as profound, is evidenced

TABLE 1.6
Number and Percentage of Cohabiting Households
with Householders Aged 45 Years and Older:
1970, 1980, 1982

	1982		1980		1970	
	Number[a]	%	Number	%	Number	%
45-64 years	197	10.6	182	11.5	123	23.5
65 years and over	103	5.5	117	7.4	113	22

SOURCE: U.S. Department of Commerce (1983: 6).
a. Numbers in thousands

in the 45 to 64 years of age category. While the percentage of elderly cohabitators has decreased substantially, the number has declined less dramatically. Since the number of people aged 65 years and over has increased significantly *and* the number of elderly cohabitators has decreased slightly, the percentage of elderly cohabitators has decreased a great deal.

While cohabitation is increasing in the United States in most age groups, it appears to be declining in the elderly segment of the population. At the present time, three-fourths of the cohabitators with no children are under 45 years of age. Will the proportion of older cohabitors increase as the group under 45 years old ages? Do cohabitors marry when they get older? There is little information to answer these questions. A study (Dressel, 1980) of marriage license applicants found that 30 percent of the older applicants listed the same address on the applications. This suggests that these persons were cohabitors before they applied for a marriage license. Were they long-term cohabitors who decide to marry when they become older? Did they live together to "try out" their relationships before marriage? Research on cohabitation of older persons would provide answers to these questions. Presently, cohabitation is primarily a lifestyle of the young but it may become more frequent in future groups of elderly.

SUMMARY

Later life families refer to couples who have launched their child and are dealing with tasks associated with a contracting nuclear unit. For childless couples, a crude indicator of entrance into the later phases is age 50 years. Later life families address tasks associated with the smaller nuclear unit, retirement, declining health and death of a spouse. These families are characterized as multigenerational with a lengthy family history.

Most of older persons are or have been married. Older men are usually married and women are either married or widowed. A small percentage of older persons have never married or divorced. For some, remarriage is a viable lifestyle in later life. A small portion of older persons cohabitate and it appears that this lifestyle has decreased over the past decade.

For the most part, the study of later life families focuses on marriage or the survivors of marriages. As the nuclear family unit becomes smaller and the typical aging processes affect a person's health, later life families seek to adapt so they can continue their family relationships. While later life families deal with many changes, they continue to value the importance of family relationships.

REVIEW QUESTIONS

(1) What is the definition of later life families? Why is chronological age an unreliable indicator of later life families?

(2) Based on the census data, what are the most frequent characteristics of families in later life?

(3) What are the differences between the family situations of older men and women?

(4) Why has the proportion of cohabitating older persons decreased? Will this trend continue in the future?

SUGGESTED PROJECTS

(1) Identify and interview a later life family. Inquire about the amount of interaction between the generations. Ask the older family members about the marital situations of many of their friends. Write a profile of this later life family.

(2) Visit a senior center and ask the older persons about their family life. Develop a table of the proportions of older men and women who are married, widowed, and divorced. Discuss the implications of these differences for family relationships.

(3) Interview three couples—young married, middled-aged, and older—about later life family relationships. Ask questions to learn about the ways they think later life family relationships will change in the future. Identify factors that suggest there will be changes in these families. Discuss what these changes will mean to future later life families.

CHAPTER
2

The Married Couple

MARRIAGE IS AN IMPORTANT relationship to older people. Older men are likely to be married, and the support they receive from the marital relationship is crucial. Older women under the age of 75 years are likely to be married, and their marital relationships are characterized by mutual support. Women aged 75 years and above are likely to have been married and the memory of this relationship cannot be minimized. The marital bond developed in the early and middle years of marriage continues into the later years. A close look at older persons' marriages may provide information for younger and middle-aged couples as they consider the future of their own marriages.

This chapter discusses the quality of older marriages as well as the relationship between marital satisfaction and overall satisfaction with life. Retirement and its influence on the marital relationship is examined. The issue of the husband's intrusion into the household *after* retirement is explored as are sex roles and sexuality in later life marriages. Since some older persons marry in later life, mate selection and remarriage of older couples are reviewed. Other topics addressed include wife's age and husband's longevity, golden wedding couples, and caregiving spouses. In considering these topics *it is important to remember that most older couples have a long history of marital interaction, either in their present or previous relationship, that influences the way in which they participate in their marriage.*

MARITAL QUALITY

Although there are few data collected from the same couples over many years and the number of older couples queried in most studies is small, there are three patterns of marital quality in later life. A review of more than 25 studies (Ade-Ridder and Brubaker, 1983) revealed conflicting findings about older couples' relationships. For example, some studies found that relationships improve with time while others reported a decline in marital quality. Still others found little change in marital quality in the later years. Before each of these patterns is discussed, it is important to mention the methodological problems with research in this area. Several critiques (Schram, 1979; Rollins and Cannon, 1974; Hicks and Platt, 1970) of this research suggested that there is a need to use standardized measures, gather longitudinal data, distinguish between childless couples and those with children, and categorize the remarried by previous status (i.e., widowed or divorced). With a recognition that the research in this area is plentiful but is marked by limitations, the three patterns will be reviewed.

In this first pattern, a number of studies (Anderson et al., 1983; Miller, 1976; Smart and Smart, 1975; Orthner, 1975; Rollins and Cannon, 1974; Stinnett et al., 1972) suggested that couples experience a decline in the quality of their marriages during the middle years, and in the later years, an increase. After the children are launched, there appears to be an increase in satisfaction with marriage. Although there is an increase, marital satisfaction does not attain the high level reported by couples who have recently been married ("honeymoon period"). However, as noted below, studies of couples married fifty years or more reported high levels of marital satisfaction.

The second pattern is a gradual decline in marital quality. A decline in marital quality of older couples has been found in most studies completed before the 1960s (Hicks and Platt, 1970). For example, Pineo (1961, 1969; Dentler and Pineo, 1960) concluded a disenchantment with marriage in the later years. Marital quality was the highest in the very early months and years of marriage and gradually declined throughout the marriage. Similarly, Blood and Wolfe (1960) observed a steady decline in marital love and companionship into the later years. However, this finding has not been reported in more recent studies. For instance, Peterson and Payne (1975) stated that husbands' feelings of love reached the lowest point in their marriages after retirement.

The third pattern of findings indicated that there is little change in the marital quality as the couple moves into the later years. Most studies reported that the childrearing years are difficult (Glenn, 1975; Deutscher, 1964; Axelson, 1960) and some couples are unhappy while others are happy with their marriages (Spanier et al., 1975; Yarrow et al., 1971). As Clark and Wallin (1965) reported, couples who are happy in the middle years continued to be happy in the later years. Also, those who were unhappy continued their dissatisfaction into the later years.

Marital quality is difficult to assess in any marriage, and in later life marriages it may be more elusive. Many couples who were dissatisfied with their relationships divorced in earlier years. Therefore, the research is only looking at the surviving relationships. Also, the older couples may be reluctant to reveal unhappiness because they have a great deal of time, energy, and themselves invested in their marriages. In any case, there are at least three patterns that characterize the marital quality of older couples.

MARRIAGE, SATISFACTION
WITH MARRIAGE, AND MORALE

The relationship between overall morale and an older person's marital status and quality is not clearly established. Gubrium (1974) reported data from 210 older persons living in an urban area and found that married persons generally were more satisfied with everyday life than individuals who were divorced or widowed. Also, older persons who had never been married had more positive views of everyday life than the divorced or widowed. This suggests that becoming divorced or widowed is associated with more negative evaluations of life. Marriage appears to contribute to higher morale if one remains married. However, if and when the marriage is terminated, overall assessments of everyday life tend to be negatively influenced.

If older persons are not satisfied with their marriages, it can be hypothesized that they may not be satisfied with their lives. This hypothesis was examined by Lee (1978) with data gathered from 258 married men and 181 married women aged 60 years and older. On the average, the men and women had been married 37 years and were in relatively good health. The results indicated that there is a relationship between marital satisfaction and morale. The higher their satisfaction with marriage, the higher were their overall morale scores. This was especially true for women, suggesting that the *quality* of a marriage may be an important factor for women when considering the issue of morale. For men, however, the mere *presence* of a spouse appears to be crucial when considering morale.

The economic situation may influence the relationship between marital status and morale. A study by Hutchinson (1975) of 893 low-income elderly provided such evidence. Married individuals have higher morale than the unmarried within the low-income category, but there was no difference in marital situation and morale for the poverty-level persons. For those living at the poverty level, being married did not contribute to overall satisfaction. Just trying to survive seemed to be a concern that outweighed the influence of a marital relationship on morale. These studies suggested that the relationship between overall morale, marital status, and satisfaction is more complex than it first appears. The economic situation and other factors such as health and the history of family interaction may be important factors to consider. For example, if an older woman neither values nor is satisfied with her marital relationship, could she find satisfaction within another aspect of her life? At this point in time, research points toward a positive relationship between overall morale, being married, and satisfied with one's marriage. Future research needs to sort out the complexities and further delineate the relationship between an older person's satisfaction with marriage and overall life morale.

MARRIAGE AND RETIREMENT

Does marriage influence the timing of retirement? Does retirement influence the marital relationship? As the number of employed wives in their middle and later years increases, the timing of their retirement and their husbands' retirement becomes a complicated issue. Atchley and Miller (1983) suggested that marriage has an influence on the timing of retirement, especially for employed wives. Married women are more likely to retire *before* age 65 while unmarried women are more likely to retire *after* age 65. Older couples, especially if they are both close to retirement age (Henrette and O'Rand, 1980), may attempt to coordinate the time they retire so that they can spend retirement together. Since women tend to marry older men, this would explain why older married women retire before age 65. Consequently, marriage influences the age at which women retire.

The retirement experience differs among older couples. First, there is the situation in which only one spouse, usually the husband, has been employed and thus only one spouse retires from employment. This can be called "single" or "traditional retirement." Then there are the dissynchronized types of retirement. In the "dissynchronized-husband initially" situation, the husband retires *before* the wife. In many instances, the wife continues her employment beyond her husband's retirement. This is because the husband started his career earlier than his wife, and is, therefore, able to retire earlier. In other cases, as mentioned above, the husband is older and consequently reaches retirement age first. In the "dissynchronized-wife initially" retirement, the wife retires *before* the husband. This occurs infrequently. "Synchronized retirement" is when *both* the husband and wife were employed and are retired at the same time. This has also been called "dual retirement" (Brubaker and Hennon, 1982).

Research focusing on the relationship between retirement and later life marriage needs to keep in mind the differences, if any, among these forms of retirement experienced by older couples. To date, this has not been done. How do older couples plan their retirements if both are employed? Do older couples attempt to synchronize their retirements? How is a marital relationship affected by a "dissynchronized-husband initially retirement"?

The influence of retirement on marital quality appears to be multifaceted and the evidence is not conclusive. Atchley and Miller (1983) reported data from a sample of 208 married, middle-class couples. The median age of the husbands was 63 years and the wives was 61 years. They found that these couples placed a high value on intimacy and family ties. Further, retirement had no measureable effect on the quality of the couples' lives. These couples had vital relationships and retirement gave them the freedom to enjoy each other. Maas and Kuypers (1977) found that the family-centered men were highly involved in the family as retirees and very satisfied with retirement. Also, the older persons with interests beyond the family had higher overall life satisfaction scores. This suggests that the marital relationship may be important to feelings of satisfaction with retirement but additional relationships (e.g., friends) are influential on life satisfaction.

Another study (Fengler, 1975) of 73 wives with husbands aged 50 years and older focused on perceptions of retirement's impact on marriage. The perceptions were categorized into three groups. Approximately one-third of the wives were "pessimists." They had traditional divisions of household labor and were concerned about the excess time their husbands would have during retirement. Also, they feared an intrusion into "their domestic territory." Nearly 40 percent of the wives were "optimists." They looked forward to their husbands' retirement and foresaw no adjustment problems. To them, retirement meant time to develop an exciting new life with their spouses. The third group, the "neutralists," predicted no changes or differences when their husbands retired. These were primarily working-class women.

Just as wives may have differing perceptions of what retirement will mean for their marriages, some wives are happy their husbands retired while others are unhappy. Heyman and Jeffers (1968) queried 33 wives whose husbands had retired; 45 percent were glad and 55 percent were sorry that their husbands had retired. The unhappy wives were older, in a lower economic status, less healthy, less satisfied with life in general and particularly with their marriage. It is important to note the likelihood that patterns reported in this study and the Fengler study were established in the early or middle years of marriage. *Perhaps the primary impact of retirement is that it highlights both positive and negative qualities of within marriages.* As Medley (1977) suggested, postretirement marital adjustment is related to the marital adjustment experienced before retirement.

Retirement may have an influence on consumption patterns of older couples. McConnel and Deljavan (1983) analyzed data of 4004 older households. They concluded that retired families spent less money for necessities, more on gifts and contributions, and about the same on transportation as compared to the nonretired elderly. Thus, retirement appears to influence the way in which older couples spend money.

Ade-Ridder and Brubaker (1983) theorized that the influence retirement has on a marriage is, in part, related to the degree of support the retiree receives from his/her mate. If the retiree's positive self-concept is reinforced by his/her spouse, the marital relationship is strengthened. However, if a spouse does not provide support, the relationship will likely be weakened. To fully understand the dynamics of the marital relationships after retirement, one of the most important issues is the type of marriage the couple had *before* retirement. Although it is obvious that many older couples maintain living patterns that were established earlier in their marriages, marital history of the retired couple is a factor that is generally overlooked in the research.

RESPONSIBILITY FOR HOUSEHOLD TASKS

Who does what around the household of older married couples? After retirement, does the husband intrude into the wife's usual activities? Does a wife marry her husband for better or worse but not for lunch? Within any household there are a number of tasks that need to be completed. In many older marriages, both the husband and wife have more time to perform these tasks. In what have been known as traditional, single-earner marriages, the retired husband may be spending more time around the home than at any period in the marriage. A number of studies focus on the division of the responsibility for household tasks among older couples.

Several studies indicate that there may not be a great deal of change after retirement in the way older couples divided the responsibility for household tasks. A study (Keating and Cole, 1980) of 400 retired teachers and their wives found that husbands did not become more involved in the household activities. For the most part, the older couples continued the patterns established before they retired. The only exception was that now some wives organized their activities around their retired husbands' schedules. Szinovacz (1980) reported similar findings from a sample of 24 recently retired married women. All the women had retired within four years prior to the interview and had been employed an average of 26 years. They stated that there was little change in the division of household tasks after they retired. The wives were primarily involved in "inside" (cooking, cleaning, laundry) tasks while their husbands had responsibility for "outside" activities (taking out the garbage, garden work). A study (Brubaker and Hennon, 1982) of 62 dual-retired and 145 dual-earner women also found little change in the divisions of household tasks after retirement. However, dual-retired and dual-earner women *expected* their husbands to share more of the responsibility for household tasks after retirement. Dobson (1983) found a slight shift to more sharing and less gender-specific assignment of responsibility in a sample of 441 persons. Generally, her findings indicated that tasks shared by middle-aged couples continue to be shared in old age. Also, tasks that are assigned to either the male or female in the middle years tend to be shared more often in old age. Studies in the early to mid-1960s provide conflicting evidence. Ballweg (1967) found traditional patterns of the division of household tasks in his studies of retired and employed older men. However, Lipman (1962; 1961) reported the sharing of activities that required little specialized training (e.g., washing dishes).

For the most part, couples do not change the division of household activities after retirement. The husband's intrusion into household activities receives little support from the research. As Keith and Brubaker (1979) noted, if the husband increases his activities in household tasks after retirement, it is usually in the areas he previously held responsibility (e.g., yard work, taking out the trash). Will future couples be more likely to share household responsibility? The Brubaker and Hennon (1982) study suggested that currently employed middle-aged women expect their husbands to share more activities after retirement. However, the same study indicated that husbands do not meet these expectations. Since couples continue patterns established before they retired, it is likely that the amount of sharing in later life marriages can be predicted from the amount of sharing that is occuring in middle-aged couples. At present, there appears to be little sharing after retirement.

There may be a difference in the number of years a couple has been married. Brubaker (1985) examined data from 32 husbands and wives who were married fifty years or more. These golden anniversary couples shared many activities and, at the same time, supported the traditional divisions of household tasks. Also, they actually had responsibility for household tasks that they expected to perform. A high degree of interdependency in the divisions of household tasks by long-married couples was obvious. Couples who celebrated fifty years of marriages appear to have unique patterns of differentiation and sharing.

SEX ROLES AND OLDER COUPLES

Although there appears to be gender-specific behavior in the division of responsibility for household tasks, some research indicates that people become less gender differentiated in personality as they age. This change is manifested in two ways. First, both men and women tend to become more androgynous with age, and second, men become more expressive and women more aggressive. Gutmann (1977; 1975) argued that men have been involved in instrumental tasks throughout their lives and they are able to "recapture femininity" in later life. At the same time, women may become more aggressive with age. A theorist (Brim, 1976) suggested that men and women change so that there is an equalization of sex role characteristics. This alteration in definitions of masculinity and femininity lead to a "normal unisex of later life." Another theorist (Livson, 1983) posited that men and women mature toward androgyny. Life stage, not chronological age, is important in defining masculinity and femininity.

While there are conflicting findings, research provides some support for the theoretical perspectives which expose less gender differentiation in later life. For example, Sinnott (1977, 1982) found older men and women to be androgynous. Minnigerode and Lee (1978) and Cameron (1968, 1976) reported that older men and women made few differentiations between masculinity and femininity. A study by Dobson (1983) indicated that older couples place more importance on expressive rather than instrumental qualities. On the other hand, Puglisi (1983) and Puglisi and Jackson (1980, 1981) reported that men do not become more feminine and that male and female roles appear to be differentiated in the later years. Also, Holahan (1984) found that there are some changes toward egalitarianism in marital attitudes and, at the same time, some areas (e.g., family finances) continue to be gender differentiated.

It may be that the personality characteristics generally associated with femininity and masculinity become redefined in later life so that there is more androgyny in later life. Older people may not be as concerned about how others perceived them. Further, as spouses, they may have developed a mutually acceptable way of interacting so that they do not rely on the socially defined definitions of masculinity and femininity. However, when it comes to the completion of household tasks, it appears that older couples generally continue patterns developed earlier in their marriages. It may be that their *attitudes* toward set role issues are more androgynous but their *behaviors* are still gender specific.

SEXUALITY OF OLDER COUPLES

Sexual expression and the interest of older couples in sexual behavior have been viewed as a topic of humor within our society. In some instances, the lack of understanding about sexuality in later life has hindered the delivery of services to older persons (Pease, 1974). Although the research is inconclusive (for example, see Garza and Dressel, 1983; Robinson, 1983; Streib and Beck, 1980), several generalizations about the sexuality of older couples that can be made. First, older couples are sexual beings as reflected in interest and activity. Second, interest and participation in sexual activity is primarily linked to the desires and performance of the husband. Third, marriage is related to the participation in sexual activity for many older persons. Let us discuss each of these generalizations in more detail.

Many individuals assume that older persons are not interested and seldom engage in sexual activity. When they are interested and active, it is viewed as an unusual event. A number of studies have queried older persons about their sexual interest and expression (see Table 2.1). With age there is a general decline, but a sizable portion report continued sexual interest and activity. For example, Roberts (1980) found 50 percent of golden wedding couples were sexually active as evidenced by their participation in coitus. As might be expected, many reported an interest in sex. Newman and Nichols (1970) had similar results from a sample of 149 married persons age 60 to 93 years. More than 50 percent were sexually active, or their sexual interest continued even though

TABLE 2.1

Research on Sexual Interest and Activity of Older Persons

Study	Men	*N* Women	Total	Age	Frequency Sexual Intercourse	Interest, Urge, Thoughts About Sex	Comments
Ard (1977)	161	161	322	20-year marriages	4-5 x month	positive feelings even if decreases in sex activity over time	1955 data
Cameron (1969)	—	—	118	60+	—	fewer thoughts than young about sex	more thoughts of safety, health
Cameron and Biber (1973)	82	80	162	65+	—	decreased interest since earlier years	—
Clark and Anderson (1967)	206	229		62-94 70	50% active	—	quantity and quality changes in sex activity
DeNicola and Peruzza (1974)	53	32	83	62-81	2 x wk. (62-71 yrs.) 3 x mo. (72-81 yrs.)	—	—
Kinsey, Pomeroy, Martin, and Gebhard (1953)	—	56		61+	.6 x wk. at 60 yrs.	—	small sample
Lowenthal, Thurnher, and Chiriboga (1975)			216	retirement—60 middle-aged—54 newlywed—50 high school—52		declined in older group— men more than women noted decline	men seen as responsible for decline by both men and women

(continued)

TABLE 2.1 Continued

Study	N Men	Women	Total	Age	Frequency Sexual Intercourse	Interest, Urge, Thoughts About Sex	Comments
Newman and Nichols (1970)			149	60-94	54% sexually active 75+ less active	constancy of drive even with decreased activity and drive strength	75+ spouse sickness activity-decrease men = reason
Pfeiffer, Verwoerdt, and Davis (1974)	261	241	502	45-71	men women none 12% 44% 1 x mo. 34% 27% 1 x wk. 41% 22% 2-3 x wk. 12% 6% 3+ x wk. 1% 1%	men women none 6% 33% mild 26% 27% moderate 56% 37% strong 12% 3%	—
Pfeiffer, Verwoerdt, and Wang (1970)	—	—	39	over 10 yrs. 67-77 mean	44% active, declined to 20% active 10 years later	60% interested over 10 yrs. men more than women	—
Roberts (1979-1980)	50	50	100	79 mean	50% active	strong interest maintained	
Verwoerdt, Pfeiffer, and Wang (1970)	—	—	254	60-94 70 median	60 yr. olds—steady 70 yr. olds—decreased activity	sustained interest to 75 yrs. interest exceeds activity.	usually reason for decrease in activity is with husband

they did not participate in sex. Many of the data on the sexuality of older couples come from the Duke Longitudinal Study (Pfeiffer et al., 1970, 1974; Newman and Nichols, 1970). Palmore (1981) reviewed these data on married couples and concluded that (1) both men and women decline in sexual participation with age (50 percent of women active to age 70 and 50 percent of men to age 70); (2) even for the active couples, frequency declines with age; (3) very few had no sexual expression; and (4) sexual interest is generally higher than sexual activity for most older couples. The research clearly indicates that older couples experience a decline in sexual interest and activity with age but they continue to be sexual beings into the later years. Many older persons are interested in sexual expression as well as being sexually active.

Husbands, more frequently than wives, are pivotal in determining the sexual activity of older couples. Garza and Dressel (1983) noted that husbands are more likely to take responsibility for the decrease in sexual activity and wives usually blame their husbands for the decline. Robinson (1983) also observed that men have more physiological limitations which may affect sexual activity in older couples. The marital partner's health is important to the participation in sex. Many times, the older couple ceases sexual intercourse as a result of a health problem. In many of these cases, sexual activity can be resumed after the health situation improves. However, the older couple may not be aware that they can participate in and enjoy sex *after* problematic health improves.

For some older persons, being married is an important requisite for sexual activity. Marriage is prerequisite to sexual activity for many older women. Robinson (1983: 89) noted that "a marriage partner is considered necessary for the sexual expression of most of today's older women, *but most older women are not married*" (emphasis added). The fact that men do not live as long as women and the social norm that men marry younger women combine to limit the opportunities for many older women to experience sex. After the death of a husband, there are two factors that are related to a wife's continued sexual activity (Corby and Zarit, 1983). One is her ability to achieve orgasm during the sexual experience and the other is her religious faith. However, for the current group of older people, marriage is important because it provides an acceptable opportunity for sexual expression.

It is important to remember two observations from the research on sexuality in later life. One, sexual expression is not limited to intercourse. Older couples are sexually active in ways that do not culminate in coitus. Touching, caressing, and massaging can be expressions of sexual desires. For some older couples, just being in bed together is a rewarding sexual experience. The closeness and warmth felt in this situation provides sexual fulfillment for some elderly husbands and wives. Seldom are these forms of sexual expression considered in the research. To fully understand the sexuality of older couples, sexual expression needs to be more broadly defined. The second observation is that the patterns of sexual expression in later life can be predicted from the patterns established in the middle years. Couples who have an active sexual relationship in the middle years can be expected to continue this relationship into later life. If a middle-aged couple has discontinued or seldom participates in sex, there is little indication that they will frequently engage in sex when they get older.

A LOOK AT GOLDEN WEDDING COUPLES

Couples who celebrate their fiftieth wedding anniversary are survivors in two ways. First, they have stayed married to the same person for fifty years. With the current divorce rate and lifespan, it is not surprising that no more than 3 percent of all marriages attain a golden wedding anniversary (Parron and Troll, 1978). Demographers Glick and Norton (1977) estimated that one in every five first marriage achieves the fifty-year status. The second indicator of survivorship is that these couples have lived long enough to achieve fifty years of marriage. Longevity is related to achievement of a golden wedding anniversary. Many individuals are denied this celebration because their spouse did not live long enough to attain fifty years of marriage. Even though some persons are postponing the age at which they first marry, this group of survivors may enlarge in the future. As persons live longer, the possibility of being married fifty years increases. Even if a person divorces and remarries, a golden anniversary may be celebrated. For example, if a person marries at age 20, divorces three years later and remarries at age 25, a golden anniversary can be celebrated at age 75 if a divorce or death does not terminate the second marriage. Golden wedding couples have beat the odds in many ways, and their marriages may provide insights into the special ingredients for a long-term relationship.

Couples married fifty or more years tend to be very satisfied with their relationships. Sporakowski and Hughston (1978) interviewed 40 couples who had been married 50 to 68 years with an average length of marriage of nearly 53 years. These persons were very satisfied with their marital relationships. The most satisfying periods in their lives had been the childbearing, preschool, and aging years. The least satisfying periods has been the childbearing, launching, and middle years. It is interesting that the childbearing years are marked with both positive and negative aspects. In another study of 50 couples married an average of nearly 56 years, Roberts (1979-1980) reported very high levels of marital adjustment. Similar to the Sporakowski and Hughston study, husbands scored higher than wives on the Locke-Wallace Marital Adjustment index. In general, long-term couples are happy with their relationships.

The high levels of happiness and adjustment reported by these couples may be a result of the types of marriages they have developed. Companionship is a key element in these marriages. Roberts found that these couples had little desire to dominate one another, and Sporakowski and Hughston's couples believed that "give and take" and "working together" were elements that made a marriage work. Parron and Troll (1978) interviewed 22 golden wedding couples and reported that sharing characterized the relationships. Generally, the couples shared household and leisure activities. The later years provided these couples with more time and opportunities to share and be together. Accommodation and companionship are two ingredients that marked the golden wedding couples. Parron and Troll posited that these factors existed throughout the couples' marriages because there appeared to be little change in the types of marriage with retirement.

The continuity of marital patterns underscores the need to examine the couple relationship over the family life cycle. Golden wedding couples have a rich marital history that can provide glimpses of the dynamics of marriage during various periods of family life. They are the survivors who may define the multiple factors that contributed to their happy relationship. Parron and Troll (1978: 462-463) were

> struck simultaneously with the simplicity of something that works and the complexity of how it has been engineered. The marital relationship of golden wedding couples during their postretirement years is an excellent opportunity to view a rare design for living.

WIFE'S AGE AND HUSBAND'S LONGEVITY

Some research suggests that it may be advantageous for a man to be married to a younger woman. Three studies of longevity patterns of married men indicated that men live longer if they are married to younger women. An analysis (Rose and Bell, 1971) of 500 deceased men who had lived in an urban area found that the more active and healthy men had younger wives. Fox and associates (1979) reported that men with spouses 5 to 10 years younger than themselves had the lowest mortality rate when compared to other age groups ranging from 15 to 74 years. Foster et al. (1984) examined deceased men aged 50 to 79 years. Husbands in all age groups who were married to younger wives had lower mortality rates. Standard mortality rates have been calculated for various age groups. A standard mortality rate of 100 means that the number of observed deaths equals the number of expected deaths (Foster et al., 1984). The standard mortality rate for men aged 50 years with younger wives was 90 while the same aged men with older wives has a rate of 112. For 70-year-old men, the respective morality rates were 80 and 133. Although the reasons are not known, there is a clear relationship between the age of the wife and the husband's length of life.

MATE SELECTION IN LATER LIFE

As reviewed in Chapter 1, some older persons remarry in later life. What factors are associated with the selection of another marital partner? Research has focused on the homogeneity (e.g., age and social class) and close geographical proximity of young newlyweds. However, little attention has been directed toward characteristics associated with mate selection of older people.

Dressel (1980) compared marriage license applications of individuals aged 65 years and over (N = 106) with those of persons aged 18 to 26 (N = 192). Of younger and older couples 99 percent were of homogeneous race. Most younger (85 percent) people married someone whose previous marital status was similar to theirs. Older persons differed significantly from younger couples in that they more frequently married individuals with differing marital histories. Generally, the younger and older samples were similar on residential propinquity—that is, choosing mates who live nearby. However, there was a tendency for older people to select marital partners who lived farther apart when compared to the younger individuals. In terms of age, older people were less likely to marry someone near their own age. Older and younger men were likely to marry younger women. The lack of homogeneity is evidenced as follows: "The older the man is, the more likely he is to marry a much younger woman, and the older a woman is, the more likely she is to marry a younger man" (Dressel, 1980: 393). This study suggests that older people are more heterogeneous in the selection of mates than are younger persons. Older people may have more opportunity to meet people of different marital backgrounds, geographical locations, and ages.

REMARRIAGE IN LATER LIFE

Although a small portion of older men and women remarry, it is an important event for those who do so. Little research has been directed toward remarriage in later life. One study (McKain, 1972; 1969) focused on 100 older couples who remarried in later life. The primary findings are that the couples were very satisfied with their new marriages. Many were attracted toward remarriage because they had felt lonely after the death of their previous spouse. Companionship is an important need that was met by the remarriage. McKain noted that it was important to discuss the remarriage with adult children and their support can enhance the new relationship. Also, he observed that it was beneficial to move into a new residence rather than move into the former residence of either the husband or wife. Remarriage provided a way for these couples to deal with their feelings of loss after the death of a spouse.

Another study of 24 elderly remarried couples (Vinick, 1978) provided similar results. The husbands and wives stated that they were satisfied with their new relationships and found remarriage to be a viable alternative to living alone. Compared to the women, the men appeared to have had more difficulty living alone after the death of a spouse. They had felt lonely and remarriage was a way to reduce these feelings. Many of the individuals had known each other prior to the death of their spouses and more than half married in less than a year from the time they started their relationships. Like McKain's couples, most married as a result of their need for companionship. There was

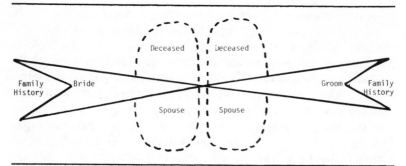

Figure 2.1: Complexity of Marital Relationship of Remarried Older Persons

little opposition from children of the older persons and most had discussed the remarriage with their children before they finalized their decision. The only negativism resulted from other older people with whom they were acquainted. Their older friends felt abandoned and jealous because the new relationships precluded their friendships. After remarriage, their friends became more supportive of their relationships. Vinick concluded that remarriage is a viable lifestyle for many older persons.

Remarriage for older persons is a complex event because both the husband and wife have a long prior family history. Many have children and grandchildren who may approve or disapprove of the new relationship. It should be recalled that many elderly remarriages involved widowed persons. Moss and Moss (1980) viewed the remarriage of an elderly widow as a triadic relationship. Unlike first marriages in which the couple is seen as a dyad, "the new marriage is viewed through the prism of the first marriage" (Moss and Moss, 1980: 66). The triad includes the elderly widowed person (male or female), new spouse, and deceased spouse. The complexity increases in remarriages that include widows and widowers (see Figure 2.1). It is assumed that the widowed person does not forget the deceased spouse and interaction in the new relationship is influenced and evaluated by the memory of the former marriage. It is difficult to share the past without comparing the present. The former can be supportive and the latter threatening to the new relationship. Remarried persons, children, and friends, need to be sensitive to the complexity of a remarriage in later life. Family history is important to retain, and it could enhance the new marital relationship.

SPOUSES AS CAREGIVERS

As a couple ages, there is an increased probability that one of the spouses will become a caregiver for the other. This is particularly the situation for individuals aged 75 years and above. As the person ages and health declines so that participation in daily activities becomes a problem, the spouse usually becomes the one who provides care. In many couples, the amount and scope of the care are extraordinary. The spouse may become the primary caregiver to someone who has difficulty walking. Or, problematic health may necessitate a special diet. In any case, the spouse with the better health condition becomes the primary caregiver. Wives, more often than husbands, are the primary caregivers (Shanas, 1979a). For example, Lopata (1973) found that nearly half of the widows she studied reported that they provided care for their husbands before their deaths. This care was provided in the home and most had been caregivers for more than a year. For some older wives, a long-term marriage is culminated with a period of caring for a husband with a debilitating health problem.

The demands of the caregiving role and changes in the marital relationship combine to create a difficult situation for the wife. Fengler and Goodrich (1979) interviewed twelve working-class wives of disabled husbands aged 65 to 85 years. The wives were 59 to 81 years old. Most of the husbands had problems that affected their mobility, senses, and use of limbs, and many had multiple problems. Both husbands and wives had lower levels of morale than have been found in other studies of nondisabled couples. Wives stated that they were worried, frustrated, saddened, resigned, and impatient with their husbands' health conditions. Role overload was found in most of the wives and especially in the group of wives who were employed. One wife remarked that "demands are constant" (p. 179). Also, they felt isolated from friends and acquaintances. Children were important social supports to the caregiving wives. As a result of these interviews, Fengler and Goodrich (1979) referred to the caregiving wives as the "hidden patients." It is clear that not all wives should provide care for their disabled husbands and wives need to assess whether they can provide the needed support.

Some older people must decide whether they should continue to care for a disabled spouse in the home or seek institutional care. Again, the disabled spouse is usually the husband. Locker (1981) discussed support groups for institutionalized older couples. Two groups of couples needed attention. One group included couples in which both the husband and wife were institutionalized. The other focused on couples in which one spouse was institutionalized and the other lived in the community. Both groups needed to address several issues. One issue was the separation from family and friends in the community when a move to an institution is made. The change to a new location was another issue because many of the couples had not moved from their homes in recent years. Finally, both groups were concerned about developing a new lifestyle. The well spouses felt a loss of emotional support and a marital partner because marital roles could no longer be fulfilled. They felt guilt about moving their ill spouse into the institution, anxiety about their own health, loneliness, and worried about finances and the need to readjust to the new situation. These older couples needed support from family, friends, and the institution to help them adjust to their new lifestyle.

Although there is an acknowledgment of the need to support care-givers, more research and the development of practical programs are needed. Possible research questions include: How does a couple make the decision to stay in a home setting or move to an institution? What impact do caregiving responsibilities have on satisfaction with a marriage? How is a spouse redefined by the caregiver? How do other family members help the caregiving spouse? Also, the development of applied programs such as support groups for caregiving spouses are important. Crossman et al. (1981) discussed a multiservice program designed to help these caregivers. The services included support groups, respite care, home care, and community education. Springer and Brubaker (1984) developed a number of exercises caregiving spouses can use to assess the caregiving situation as well as other resources that may be helpful. More projects and materials are needed to assist the caregiving spouse.

SUMMARY

Marriage is a viable way of life for many older persons. Many have been married for a number of years and are satisfied with their relationships. After the children leave home, the marital relationship seems to improve, and for some, retirement provides the time to spend together as spouses. Hence, marriage is a source of rewards and supports for an older couple as they age. It is likely that both the launching of the children and retirement exacerbate long-standing problems in some marriages. Little research has focused on older persons who have unhappy marriages. As the longevity rates increase, the number of long-term marriages is likely to increase—It will not be uncommon for persons to be married 50 to 60 years. These survivors provide an interesting group of older marriages. Also, as more men and women are employed throughout their lives, the number of "dual-retired" couples will increase. Since spouses continue patterns of interaction into the later years, research on older couples would benefit all aged couples.

REVIEW QUESTIONS

(1) What is the quality of older persons marriages? Is there a relationship between marital quality and satisfaction with life in general? What are important factors related to the marital quality of older couples?

(2) How does retirement influence an older couple's marital relationship?

(3) How do older couples divide responsibility for household tasks? Do older couples change the divisions of household responsibility as they age?

(4) How do you characterize the sexuality of older couples?

(5) Why are golden anniversary couples unique?

(6) What are some of the problems associated with mate selection and remarriage in later life?

(7) Who are the "hidden patients" and what support do they need?

SUGGESTED PROJECTS

(1) Interview an older, retired couple about the changes they have had in the past few years. Ask them about the changes since retirement. Discuss the ways they divide household activities.

(2) Older couples have different family situations and relationships. Write two or three profiles to illustrate differences between couples. For example, one couple may have been married for 45 years and have no children. Another couple may be married two years after both had been widowed. Discuss the different challenges they face and ways they deal with problems.

(3) Interview a couple married 50 years or more. Ask them to describe their marriage and comment on criteria for long-term relationships. What advice do they have for newly married couples?

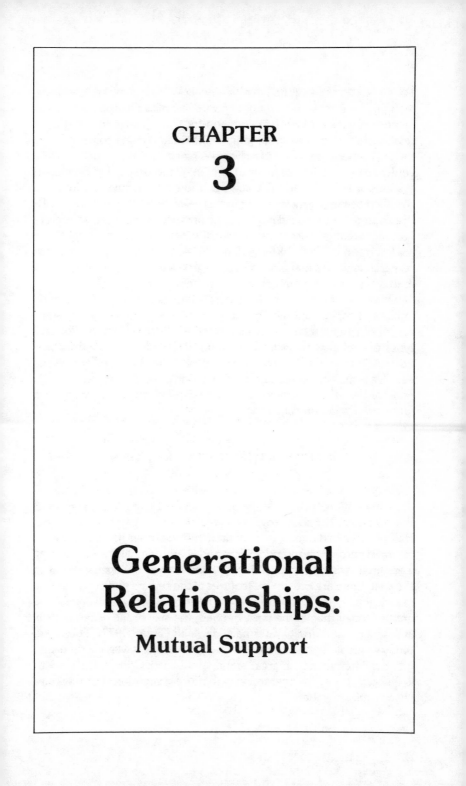

CHAPTER
3

Generational
Relationships:
Mutual Support

TODAY'S LATER LIFE FAMILIES have been called "new pioneers" because many include more generations than did families at the turn of the century (Shanas, 1980). It is common for older people to experience relationships with their great-grandchildren, and many come to know the fifth generation of their families. As pioneers, these families "have ventured into uncharted areas of human relationships, and developed systems of exchange and interaction without help or guidance from the so-called helping agencies in our industrial society" (Shanas, 1980: 14). Previous generations did not have the opportunity to observe interaction with great-grandparents or even grandparents. Even though there are few role models and little guidance for these family relationships, the research indicates that older and younger generations have negotiated mutually satisfying intergenerational relationships.

This chapter focuses on the generational relationships with later life families. The size and age of the generations, younger generations' responsibility for older generations, and frequency of interaction and types of exchange between generations will be discussed. Other sections include a focus on providing support to dependent older persons who live in multigenerational households and in institutions. Research is reviewed on the generational relationships of childless elderly and future trends are presented.

SIZE AND AGE OF GENERATIONS

As noted, the majority of older people have children and grandchildren. In a national probability sample, Shanas (1980; 1979a, b) reported that 80 percent of people over 65 years and older have living children. Half of these had one or two children and the other half had three or more; 94 percent had grandchildren and nearly one-half stated that they were great-grandparents. Although families were multigenerational in the past, there are two unique features of the current pioneers. First, as noted above, the probability of four- or five-generation families is greater today than in the past. Second, the size of the generations is smaller because fertility rates have declined (Treas, 1977). Therefore, today's middle-aged parents are likely to have fewer children and grandchildren than their great-grandparents had. Consequently, there is an opportunity for interaction with more generations but there are fewer family members.

The implications of more generations with fewer members have not been clearly identified. Treas (1977) noted that fewer children may mean that there are fewer family members to help older persons when they need assistance. However, the smaller size of the generations may contribute to the development of closer, more intimate relationships (Hess and Waring, 1978). Although intergenerational families are smaller, the interactions between the generations may be based on strong affectional bonds and characterized by mutual respect.

In a description of older parent-child relationships, variability in the ages of the generations should not be overlooked. While most older people's children are middle-aged, some have children who are over 65 years of age, some have adolescent children while a few have preschool children (Cicirelli, 1983b). Although there may be some differences between the parental-child relationships of older people with younger or middle-aged children, no research has focused on this issue.

FILIAL RESPONSIBILITY

Filial responsibility refers to adult children's feelings that they *should* help their elderly parents. When an elderly parent is in need of assistance their children may feel that a responsibility, and at times, a sense of duty to help them (Schorr, 1960). The children may visit, perform household chores or, in some cases, hire someone to help their elderly parents. This type of parent-child interaction is an indication of a mature relationship. Blenkner (1965) discussed filial maturity as a part of a developmental aspect of the relationship between parents and children. As parents and children age, children mature and recognize that their parents are dependent and need their help. As children mature in the relationship with their parents, they feel a responsibility to provide assistance to their aging parents. For example, a daughter whose mother is a nursing home resident may accept her mother's need for emotional support and visit her regularly. Or, a daughter-in-law may grocery shop for her mother-in-law on a weekly basis.

The bond between older parents and their children may be strengthened by feelings of obligation, mutual respect, or affection. For some, it may be that their mutual needs attract a reciprocal relationship. The older parents help their adult children and, in turn, the adult children care for the parents. Although the content of the parent-child relationship is not clearly defined and some confusion has been identified (Johnson, 1981), both generations expect reciprocity to characterize their interactions.

Research reveals evidence that children feel some obligation to help dependent parents. Several studies (Cicirelli, 1983a; Schlesinger et al., 1980; Seelbach, 1978; Seelbach and Sauer, 1977) found that adult children expect to help their older parents. The daughters have stronger feelings of filial responsibility than do sons. Black and white adult children reported similar feelings of filial responsibility in these studies, although actions may vary.

Other studies indicate that there are some conflicting findings on racial differences of filial responsibility. For example, Hanson et al. (1983) found that whites scored higher on the filial responsibility measures than blacks. Sanders and Seelbach (1981) reported that whites were more likely than blacks to desire assistance from family rather than nonfamilial sources. In any case, there is support that both white and black adult children and their parents seek the family as a significant source of assistance.

Development of filial maturity as a result of the affection and intimacy of the parent-child relationships has been the focus of research. Present helping behavior, feelings of attachment to parents, and contact with parents are related to a commitment to provide help in the future (Cicirelli, 1983a). Therefore, if adult children have been helping their parents, it is likely that they will continue to do so. Also, if the children had a close relationship and frequent contact with their parents, they were likely to provide help in the future. However, in contrast to Cicirelli's findings, one study (Walker and Thompson, 1983) of mothers and daughters reported that intimacy was not related to exchanges of aid and interaction. Research indicates that there are intergenerational feelings of responsibility, intimacy, and affection, but the reasons for these feelings are not clear.

FREQUENCY OF INTERACTION

It is evident that older people have children and grandchildren with whom to interact but the amount of interaction between the generations is the crucial issue. Shanas (1979a) found that 50 percent of the men and 54 percent of the women had seen one of their children the day of or the day before the interview. Another 23 percent of the men and 25 percent of the women stated that they had seen at least one child within the week before the interview. Only 13 percent of the men and 9 percent of the women had not seen one child for more than a month. Generally, the research on the frequency of intergenerational contact indicates that most (80 to 90 percent) of older people have frequent contact with their children. This contact, depending on the location of the children, includes face-to-face visits or telephone conversations.

Older people and their children have developed strong bonds which encourage them to continue interaction throughout the family life cycle. One study (Cicirelli, 1981a) found that approximately nine out of ten adult children sampled felt "close" or "very close" to their older fathers and mothers. Only 2 percent of the adult children stated that they felt "not close at all" to their elderly fathers and none felt this way toward their mothers. In the same study, the adult children were asked about the conflict they had with their older parents. Only 6 percent had frequent conflict with their fathers and 5 percent had frequent conflict with their mothers. More than one-third of the respondents had no conflict with their mothers or fathers. Both institutionalized and community-dwelling elderly are ordinarily satisfied with their family relationships (Seelbach and Hanson, 1980). They do not feel abandoned or neglected by their children. Three-fourths of the institutionalized elderly perceived themselves as receiving as much love as ever.

Differences between the intergenerational patterns of white and black families have been the focus of a number investigations. Some scholars have argued that the black elderly are a part of an extended family network (Hill, 1978; Jackson, 1972a, 1972b). One study (Dowd and Bengtson, 1978) indicated the older blacks and Mexican-Americans had more frequent contact with their children and grandchildren than did elderly whites. More recently, Mitchell and Register (1984) examined data of 334 black and 1,813 white elderly from the national survey conducted by Louis Harris and Associates for the National Council on Aging. They found that there is no difference in the frequency with which black and white elderly see their children and grandchildren: 77 percent of the white elderly and 81 percent of the black elderly had seen their children with the last 2 weeks. Seventy-three percent of the whites and 74 percent of the blacks had seen their grandchildren with the same period.

The location of the children has been found to be an important factor in the frequency of the contacts of urban, older blacks (Wolf et al., 1983) and whites (Hays, 1984). Elderly, urban blacks with children living in the same neighborhood had contact with their children an average of 24 times per month while those with children living in other parts of the city (within a one-hour drive) had an average of 11 contacts per month. Consequently, black extended families in an urban setting visit with one another more frequently when they live close to one another.

Older people and their children and grandchildren have developed relationships characterized with frequent contact. While there is a small portion of elderly who have little or no contact with their children or grandchildren, it is clear that most have a pattern of interaction. This intergenerational relationship is based on a long history of family inter-action and there is no reason for the relationship to be altered when the parents become older. If frequency of interaction is used as an indication of an extended family network, both black and white elderly are members of a vibrant, extended family.

TYPES OF EXCHANGES

Older parents and their adult children interact by providing assistance when illness occurs, giving emotional support and expert guidance as well as helping each other with various household tasks. When an older person becomes ill and cannot take care of the housework, prepare meals or shop, adult children are likely to provide assistance (Shanas, 1979a). Grandchildren may mow the lawn or shovel snow from the sidewalks. Grandparents may take care of grandchildren so that the parents can have a respite from their childrearing responsibilities. There are numerous ways by which the generations exchange aid. A common finding in the research on intergenerational exchanges is that older people first turn to their families when they need assistance and, most times, the families provide the assistance.

The Mitchell and Register (1984) study noted above illustrates the mutual exchanges between the generations. Older people stated that they received help when they were ill and they helped their children or grandchildren when they experienced illness. Also, they stated that children or grandchildren ran errands for them, took them places (e.g., church, doctor), and repaired things around the house. All generations were least likely to give advice on money matters and matters dealing with a job or business. The Mitchell and Register analysis suggested that elderly blacks received more assistance from their children and grandchildren than elderly whites. Further, elderly blacks were more likely to ask other relatives (children, grandchildren, nieces, nephews) to move into their homes than elderly whites, regardless of their socioeconomic status. The amount of help an older person gives to children or grandchildren was related to the socioeconomic level of the elderly blacks and whites. Elderly of lower socioeconomic standing were more likely to give assistance than those of higher socioeconomic status. The persons with the least resources were more likely to provide assistance to their children or grandchildren. Elderly blacks and whites participate in an exchange of interactions between the generations and the exchange includes various types of activities of support.

The types of assistance families provide older family members may differ depending on the formal supports available. Older blacks receive more assistance from the formal support system in basic maintenance areas (e.g., financial aid, food, groceries, housing) than do elderly whites (Mindel, 1983). However, the elderly blacks receive more assistance from the informal support system in the area of home and personal care (e.g., nursing care, meals, supervision). Also, there may be differences between other minority groups in generational exchanges. Weeks and Cuellar (1981) examined the exchange patterns of older persons representing various minority groups. The groups included Hispanic, black, Filipino, Samoan, Guamanian, Japanese, Chinese, Korean, and American Indian. They found that persons of an Asian (including Pacific Islanders) background were more likely to turn to family members for assistance than were the other minority groups. Immigrants were likely to rely on the family for help while native-born persons tended to turn to nonfamily assistance. Evidence suggests that the exchanges between the generations may differ as a result of the minority or ethnic subculture.

Another influence on adult child-parent interaction may be the employment status of the adult children. For example, an unemployed daughter may be able to spend a great deal of time each day with her parents while an employed daughter may be limited in the time she devotes to her parents. Treas (1977) observed that more adult daughters and daughters-in-law are employed outside the home than in previous years. Since women provide most of the care for older dependent family members (Newman, 1976), the increase in women's employment may compete with the ability to care for an older family member. However, the employed adult children may be able to pay for the assistance they would have provided if they were not employed or they may choose to reduce their working time.

A recent study (Stoller, 1983) examined the competition of adult children's employment and their provision of assistance to their older parents. The sample included noninstitutionalized elderly and their adult sons and daughters who were informal helpers. The findings indicate that adult children provide less assistance if a spouse is present in the older persons home. Daughters and sons note that their own marriage relationships compete with the time they spend helping their parents. Contrary to Treas's (1977) prediction, employment does not significantly affect the number of hours a daughter spent providing assistance to elderly parents. However, employment significantly reduced the amount of time sons devote to assisting their older parents. These data suggest that the daughters, even though they are employed, arrange their schedules to provide assistance to their parents. As Brody (1981) suggested, adult daughters are "women in the middle" because they are pulled to fulfill their parental and marital responsibilities to their children and husbands and, at the same time, propelled by the feelings of filial maturity to provide assistance to their elderly parents.

Does the mutual exchange between the generations contribute to an older person's satisfaction with life? It might be argued that older persons feel positive about helping their children and are gratified when their children help them. Cheal (1983) theorized that the older generation's obligation to transfer resources to the younger generation is stronger than the younger generation's obligation to transfer resources to the older. It follows that the older parents would feel more satisfied with their life situation if they can provide aid to their children. However, Lee and Ellithorpe (1982) found that older persons' satisfaction with life was not enhanced by the ability to provide assistance to, or receive help from their children. It was suggested that the aid the older persons provided may drain resources from the older parents need, and consequently, their overall morale was not increased.

One recent study (Cicirelli, 1983c) compared the helping patterns of 141 adult children from disrupted marriages (i.e., divorced, widowed, remarried) and 164 adult children from intact marriages. Adult children from disrupted marriages provided less, *but not drastically less*, help than children from intact marriages. The primary interference to providing help was the competition from employment demands. Job responsibilities were particularly high among divorced women. This study suggested that adult children's marital situation has limited effect on the help provided to older parents.

The research clearly indicates that there is a vital, supportive network of exchanges developed by older persons and their children and grandchildren. The ways in which these patterns of mutual exchanges occur may vary and we do not fully understand the motivations of the participants in the exchange. We do know that it is working well, although the cost in terms of money (J. Montgomery, 1982), time, and energy to families is extraordinary. Future research needs to explore the reasons family members provide this assistance and ways to give more support to these families. Identifying ways to mesh family resources and skills with bureaucratic resources and skills to meet the needs of the older persons is a major task for researchers and policymakers.

MULTIGENERATIONAL HOUSEHOLDS

Multigenerational households refer to situations in which older persons are living with adult children and/or grandchildren under the same roof. In most instances, these households are formed after the adult children and have moved out of their parent's house. Later, either the older generation moves into a child's residence or the adult child returns to parental house. The households may include two, three, and in a few instances, four generations. Since a few of the cases comprise families in which the adult children never moved out of the parents' house, some of the multigenerational households have had a long history of interaction.

Data from the U.S. Bureau of the Census indicate several trends in multigenerational households (Shanas, 1980; Mindel, 1979). First, most older men and women live independently of their children and other relatives. Second, there has been a substantial decline in the number of households in which young married children live with their parents since the early 1900s. For example, the percentage of married couples living with their parents ("doubling up") has declined from 5.4 percent in 1910 to 1.2 percent in 1978 (Mindel, 1979). Third, the percentage of older men and women living with their children or other relatives has declined by at least 50 percent in the past 35 years. Fourth, the primary impetus for multigenerational households is to prevent the entrance of an older parent into a institution (e.g., nursing home). Although some elderly fathers do so, this living arrangement especially applies to older, single women (Mindel, 1979). It should also be noted that multigenerational households are likely to include older persons above age 75 years and who experience health difficulties.

Interaction in a multigenerational household may be satisfying and rewarding and, at the same time, very stressful. Mindel and Wright (1982) analyzed the adult child-parent relationship of 99 multigenerational households. Interviews were conducted with 99 elderly persons and their primary caregivers (usually, daughters or daughters-in-law). Caregiver satisfaction was related to the level of inconvenience the older person created in the household as well as the older person's level of activity. Level of activity was also related to the amount of inconvenience because the more active older persons participated in the household chores and thereby were not seen as creating an inconvenience. The never-married and black caregivers had higher family satisfaction scores than the married and white caregivers. This study suggested that the level of satisfaction is affected by the costs the families assess to the presence of the older person. If the older person does not interrupt the family routines or the completion of family tasks the caregiving generation is satisfied with the multigenerational household. However, if disruption characterizes the relationship, satisfaction is diminished.

There are a number of factors that may reduce the possibility of stress in a multigenerational household. Brubaker and Brubaker (1981) theorized that structural (e.g., gender of person, family composition, social class), individual family member (e.g., type of dependency, filial maturity, attitudes toward aging), family (e.g., coping skills, family history) and community resource (e.g., financial, transportation, adult day care centers) factors interrelate to affect the level of stress experienced within multigenerational households. These factors are presented in Figure 3.1. It is important to recognize that some families may function well as multigenerational households while others have difficulties. For example, if a family has a history of problematic interaction between an adult child and older parent, it is likely that a multigenerational household will exacerbate the difficulties. If, however, a family copes well with stress and is prepared to use community resources to meet the needs of the older person, a multigeneration household may be a rewarding situation.

The development of stress within a multigenerational family is related to the family's feelings of burden. Poulshock and Deimling (1984) reported data from a study of 614 families who either lived with or care for dependent, older family members. The findings indicated that

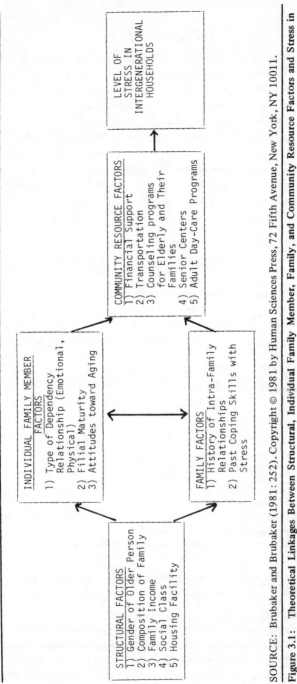

STRUCTURAL FACTORS
1) Gender of Older Person
2) Composition of Family
3) Family Income
4) Social Class
5) Housing Facility

INDIVIDUAL FAMILY MEMBER FACTORS
1) Type of Dependency Relationship (Emotional, Physical)
2) Filial Maturity
3) Attitudes toward Aging

FAMILY FACTORS
1) History of Intra-Family Relationships
2) Past Coping Skills with Stress

COMMUNITY RESOURCE FACTORS
1) Financial Support
2) Transportation
3) Counseling programs for Elderly and Their Families
4) Senior Centers
5) Adult Day-Care Programs

LEVEL OF STRESS IN INTERGENERATIONAL HOUSEHOLDS

SOURCE: Brubaker and Brubaker (1981: 252). Copyright © 1981 by Human Sciences Press, 72 Fifth Avenue, New York, NY 10011.

Figure 3.1: Theoretical Linkages Between Structural, Individual Family Member, Family, and Community Resource Factors and Stress in Intergenerational Households

feelings of burden are subjectively defined by the caregivers and mediate the relationship between objective factors and the level of impairment. Thus, family caregivers view their relationship with their dependent older person on an individualized level.

The decision to form a multigenerational household is one that can only be made by the family members involved. Some families may experience a positive relationship with many benefits for each generation. However, other families may continue a deterioration begun many years ago. Individuals who are considering the possibility of forming a multigenerational household may want to answer the questions presented in Table 3.1. Multigenerational households are a unique living

TABLE 3.1

Important Questions When Considering the Formation of a Multigeneration Household

Adult children may need to consider whether they want to form a multigenerational household with their older parents. To make a rational decision, it is important to ask yourself the following questions:

Getting to know your *feelings* about caring for the older parent:
(1) How do you feel about helping your older parents?
      Do you owe them something just because they raised you?
(2) How do you feel about old age? Do you see your parents as old?
(3) What needs do your parents have, and how can you meet these needs?

Getting to know your *family:*
(1) What is your relationship with your parents? Do you get along well with them? Are you close to them?
(2) How does your family deal with illness or financial problems?
      Do they come together and help each other, feel resentment, or what?

Getting to know your *situation:*
(1) Will everyone have enough privacy?
(2) Will you have to do any remodeling, such as wheelchair ramps, railings?
(3) Is there enough room in your house?
(4) Will there be enough money when all the resources are pooled?

Getting to know your community *resources:*
(1) Does your community have a transportation program for elderly?
(2) Is there a senior center near your home?
(3) Is there an adult day care center?
(4) Is there a respite program at a local nursing home?
(5) Are home-delivered meals available?
(6) Are home health care, telephone reassurances, and housekeeping assistance services available in your community?

SOURCE: Hennon et al. (1983).

arrangement for older persons and are characterized by costs as well as rewards.

INSTITUTIONALIZED DEPENDENT FAMILY MEMBERS

Some families have older members who cannot take care of themselves and cannot be cared for within multigenerational households. These older persons reside in long-term care institutions such as nursing homes. The percentage of families who are in this situation is small. For example, less than 5 percent of people over age 65 years are living in any type of institution including hospital and nursing homes. Many of these have no family to care for them. While the proportion of families with dependent older persons in institutions is small, the burden on these families is large. It is more difficult for the generations to interact because the older persons are living in an institution. Also, many of the younger generations have misconceptions about institutional life, and their relationship with their older person is adversely affected. However, family members are interested in, and provide support for, their institutionalized members.

The younger generations continue relationships with their older relatives after a move into a nursing home. York and Caslyn (1977) studied families who had members in a nursing home setting and found that younger generations were involved with the older relatives before they entered the nursing homes. Most of the families did shopping, laundry cleaning, cooking and various other activities for the older person. Nearly 30 percent had the older person living with them. When the decision to move to a nursing home was made, the families were actively involved. However, the children did not know a great deal about how to select a nursing home and were unsophisticated in their search for placement. After entrance into the nursing home, the families continued to visit. The average number of visits was 12 per month. Other studies of the visitation patterns of three nursing homes found that most visitors are children and grandchildren (Hook et al., 1982; Spasoff et al., 1978). Of the elderly residents sampled 96 percent had relative visits in a one-month period and there was no substantial decline in the number of visits during the first year of institutionalization (Spasoff et al., 1978).

Generational interaction and support continues after a family member is institutionalized. An older person's children and grandchildren are important, and generational interaction has been associated with more positive feelings of resident well-being (Greene and Monahan, 1982; Noelker and Harel, 1978). Adult children and grandchildren need support as they continue their relationships with older relatives in institutions. The York and Caslyn study indicates that the younger generations are not knowledgeable about institutional procedures, treatment plans, or the aging processes in general. Generational involvement may be encouraged or discouraged by the policy of the institutions. For example, the degree of integration between the family (i.e., older person, adult children, and grandchildren) and the institution may vary between nursing homes (R. Montgomery, 1982). Some facilities do not have a generational view of the family and provide few services to the adult children and grandchildren. Others may define the older person *and* children and grandchildren as clients and provide services to all.

It is important for families to consider the degree to which an institution encourages generational involvement with residents before selection of a nursing home is made. It has been suggested that "the optimal care policy for enhancing family integration is one that actively recruits the family and services the family as a client" (R. Montgomery, 1982: 53).

CHILDLESS ELDERLY

While the majority of older people have living children, approximately two out of every ten elderly are childless. Childless elderly include married couples who, voluntarily or involuntarily, had no children, divorced or widowed elderly who also had no children, and the never-married persons without children. A small portion are elderly whose children have preceded them in death. Most of these elderly have been childless throughout their lives and their generational interactions have been limited as a result of the truncated family structure. When the childless become older, the natural support system of children and grandchildren is nonexistent. Often an argument used to persuade married couples to have children includes the belief that "children will take care of you in your old age." The research on adult children's support of older persons suggests that children provide a great deal of support to their older parents. Gerontological researchers have directed their attention toward the interaction patterns of and support systems available to the childless elderly.

Bachrach (1980) examined the interaction of childless elderly from a national sample. In general, it was concluded that childlessness was a predictor of social isolation in later life. Elderly with no children had fewer social contacts when compared to elderly parents. For example, one-quarter of the childless elderly had not had contact with anyone in the past couple of days, while less than 10 percent of the parental group reported no interaction in the same time period. Incidentally, the number of children an elderly person had was not related to the amount of social contact. Older people with one child were as socially active as those with several children and they were significantly more active than childless elderly. The childless elderly, in this sample, did not have more social contact with other relatives than did elderly with children.

Social isolation of the childless increases when the health of the older persons becomes problematic (Beckman and Houser, 1982; Bachrach, 1980). Consequently, the elderly who have no children have fewer social contacts as they experience more health difficulties. This study also found that the childless elderly have a higher probability of living alone. However, the living situation differs between the married and never-married childless persons. The most common alternative to living alone was living with a child or grandchild for those who had been married. For the never married, the most frequent alternative was living with a sibling or other relative. The presence of children in the family network lessens the probability of social isolation for the elderly and is particularly important when an older persons becomes physically dependent (Bachrach, 1980).

Differences exist between the marital status of childless elderly (Johnson and Catalano, 1981). Generally, the unmarrieds are less isolated than their married counterparts. The unmarried have active interaction patterns with their friends and neighbors while the married center their interaction around their marital partner. When health declines and the childless elderly needed assistance, siblings are the most important source of support. Nieces and nephews also provided assistance but their relationship is less intimate than that of the siblings. For the married, the spouses provide the help. The unmarried childless have a higher rate of institutionalization than the married childless elderly. For example, in a study of married and unmarried childless elderly, the institutionalization rate for the unmarried was 44 percent and only 17 percent for the married (Johnson and Catalano, 1981).

Within an urban setting, the social isolation of the married childless elderly may be explained by their focus on the marital relationship at the cost of developing other social relationships. Johnson and Catalano (1981) suggested that the married couples have a history of relying on one another, and consequently, their social contacts are limited. Seldom do the married use support from other sources even if a need is evident. In fact, they developed a reluctance to use formal services. However, the unmarried childless elderly expected to need help in the future and cultivated relationships for that purpose. There was a form of anticipatory socialization for the time when they can no longer care for themselves. Relatives such as siblings and formal services are requested to help and they attempt to develop a social network to assist them. Therefore, social isolation is a particular problem for married childless older persons and social interactions are more frequent for the unmarried childless elderly living in an urban area.

Findings from a sample of rural childless elderly indicated many similarities to their urban counterparts. Kivett and Learner (1980) analyzed data from 66 childless elderly and 315 older parents. Compared to the parental elderly, the older childless are more highly educated, more likely to live alone, less likely to have transportation, and use the telephone less frequently. As a group, they are more socially isolated than the older persons who had children but are not any more lonely and are as likely to have someone in whom to confide. Apparently, the childless elderly develop a social network of friends and relatives whom they trust, even though they have contact with them less frequently.

Although the childless elderly have developed supportive networks in urban and rural settings, there is some evidence that they may be less satisfied with their family situation than older persons with children (Singh and Williams, 1981). Also, they expect, and use, formal services. The married and unhealthy, unmarried childless elderly may be at risk because they are more socially isolated and their support networks are limited when compared to elderly with children. If the number of childless couples increases, the proportion of older people who are isolated and need formal assistance may grow.

FUTURE GENERATIONAL RELATIONSHIPS

Future generational relationships may be influenced by the number of children today's younger and middle-aged couples have. The overall proportion of older persons in the population and size of future family support networks is related to the fertility rates. Demographers' predictions of future fertility rates vary (Treas, 1981). Some foresee high fertility rates, which suggest that the ratio between young and old will plateau at about 14 percent (14 older persons for every 100 persons aged 64 years and less). Others predict low fertility rates and a rise to about 22 percent of the population consisting of older people by the year 2030. Low fertility rates and the resultant high portion of elderly may affect the generational relationships. Families may be strained by the small numbers of producers and the large number of dependent elderly if intergenerational transfers continue to finance older people (Treas, 1981). Stress may develop between the generations because there are fewer persons with whom to share the burden of caring for dependent older persons. While there is no certainty concerning future fertility rates, there is no doubt that the size of each generation is an important factor in generational relationships.

Generational relationships will probably be increasingly complex because they are influenced by changes within family units of each generation in a family network. Riley (1983: 443) suggested that "the longer the relationship endures (because of longevity) the greater the opportunity for relational changes." As a person ages and the family adds generations, the complexity of the relationships increase. For example, when a granddaughter marries, a grandson-in-law is added to the relational structure. If, after three years of marriage and one child, the granddaughter divorces this grandson-in-law and subsequently remarries another person, the older relative has another individual added to the family network. The elderly person may continue (but not necessarily) a relationship with the first grandson-in-law.

There is no doubt that the complexity of the generational structure of a family becomes greater as a person ages. The frequency of divorce within family networks further complicates the generational structure of older persons. Not only is there a change in the number of persons in the family network but there are few guidelines on how to interact with these individuals. In the example above the grandparent may not know how to continue a relationship with the ex-grandson-in-law because there are few societal norms defining this relationship. Future generational relationships will continue to be complex and influenced by changes within the family structure. Further, there will be a need to develop new ways of interacting within the generational structure. As Hagestad (1981: 25) argued, "Adults in intergenerational relationships may find themselves in a situation demanding negotiation skills previously not called for, since they to a large extent have to create the structure and meaning of their bond."

Since most support for dependent older family members is provided by women *and* more women are employed outside the home, the finding that employed women continue to provide assistance to older family members is important. Working women with a dependent older relative are adding another responsibility to their already increased workload. They are exceeding the responsibility of the superwomen who work and care for their husbands and children. They are also responsible for their dependent older relatives. Consequently, there may be a need to develop ways to alleviate the stresses peculiar to the employed woman who is also a primary caregiver.

SUMMARY

Mutual support characterizes most of the generational relationships of older persons. Older persons interact with their children and grandchildren. The younger and older family members expect to provide assistance to older dependent family members and research on exchange patterns between the generations indicates that these expectations are fulfilled. For the elderly who experience health difficulties, family members generally attempt to meet their daily needs. In some families, the older person becomes a member of a multigenerational household. In a few situations, the older person moves into an institution and the family continues to visit and provide support.

Given the extraordinary amounts of assistance younger generations attempt to give to their elderly family members, it is not surprising that stress characterizes some generational interactions. Family caregivers, usually women, are vulnerable to feelings of stress and overload. The childless elderly, particularly the married and unhealthy unmarried, are often socially isolated and in need of formal supports. Future generational relationships will continue to be complex and the fertility rate will probably affect the interactional patterns.

REVIEW QUESTIONS

(1) What is the importance of four and five generation families for later life family relationships?

(2) How do you describe the frequency and type of interaction between the older and younger generations within families?

(3) What are some stresses associated with multigenerational households?

(4) How are families involved with older members who are institutionalized?

(5) Who provides assistance to elderly who have no children?

SUGGESTED PROJECTS

(1) Examine your own family network and the types of interaction between the younger and older generations. How many generations are there in your family? What is the frequency and content of intergenerational contacts? How do you plan to interact with your parents when they are older?

(2) Interview persons living in a multigenerational household. What are the rewards of living in such a household? What are the stresses? What can be done to reduce stress in this situation?

(3) Visit a nursing home and talk to the staff and some of the residents about the involvement of families with their elderly members. Ask the staff about ways they try to encourage family involvement.

CHAPTER
4

Grandparents,
Siblings, and Other
Relatives

As A PERSON AGES, there are opportunities to establish new as well as to continue long-standing relationships within the family. Grandparenthood represents one of the situations in which new family relationships are created because grandparenting is a linking of older with younger generations. It is an opportunity to continue family patterns by transferring information from the more experienced to the neophyte generations. The richness of the family history includes positive aspects as well as negative features. Grandparenthood should be considered in light of the family traditions and history. Similarly, the older person's sibling relationships reverberate with the interactions of the past. The shared childhood, coveted experiences, and unique lives combine to influence sibling relationships in later life. Nieces, nephews, and for some, individuals who are not related but treated as kin are other relatives that are important to later life family patterns.

This chapter will examine the grandparents, siblings, and other relatives who contribute to family life in the later years. First, grandparenthood will be discussed. The specific topics relative to grandparenting include the value of grandparenting, becoming a grandparent, types of grandparents, grandchildren's views of grandparents, divorce and grandparenting as well as future research needs in the grandparenting area. Second, an older person's sibling relationships will be explored. Unique features of sibling relationships, feelings of closeness, gender differences, death of a sibling, and the importance of the sibling relationship are addressed. The third and final section deals with other relatives' relationships in later life families.

GRANDPARENTHOOD

Grandparenthood is a part of family life for many individuals. A national survey of people aged 65 years and over found that 75 percent had living grandchildren (Harris et al., 1975). Many individuals are grandparents before they celebrate their sixty-fifth birthday. For some people, the first grandchild arrives when they are in the early or mid-40s (Troll, 1980). Others become grandparents in the fifth or sixth decades of life. Therefore, grandparenthood is experienced by individuals of a variety of ages. An early study of grandparenting suggested that these age differences may be influence grandparenting roles (Neugarten and Weistein, 1964). Another factor is that older people may have been grandparents many years before they launched their last child or retired. For most older people, grandparent and grandchild interaction is frequent. Harris et al. (1975) reported that three-fourths of the older persons who had grandchildren had contact with them on a weekly basis.

Grandparents are in a unique position in the family network because they are not the parents of the younger generation but they have a vested interest in the development of the grandchild. Since family values and themes are continued by each subsequent generation, grandparents have a generational stake in their grandchildren (Troll, 1980). They want the grandchildren to pass on the family traditions. Generally, the grandparents do not get directly involved in the raising of their grandchildren but they express their interest at a distance (Troll, 1983). Much of their interactions with and influences on the grandchildren are mediated by the parental generation. Therefore, the grandparents are in a unique position within the family network, as they have considerable interest in but little control of the relationship. They are, as Troll (1983) suggested, the "family watchdogs."

The Value of Grandparenting

A sample of 90 grandmothers was queried about the value the grandparent-grandchild relationship had for them (Timberlake, 1980). The majority (80 percent) of grandmothers valued this intergenerational relationship because it provided a continuation of themselves through another generation. Nearly three out of five claimed that grandchildren filled a need of creativity, accomplishment, competence, and a reconfirmation of their own identity. The more involved in the grandchild's care and the more frequent the contact, the more their social identity was supported. Presumably, these grandmothers' identities were linked to their definitions of motherhood because they were more likely to confirm their identities if they frequently cared for their grandchild. In any case, grandchildren were highly valued by grandmothers for a variety of reasons.

Five meanings of grandparenthood have been identified including (1) grandparenthood as central to the older person's life, (2) grandparents seen as elders, (3) grandparenthood creates a feeling of one's immortality, (4) older person's ability to relive his/her life through grandparenting, and (5) a feeling that grandparents can indulge their grandchildren (Kivnick, 1982). Grandmothers and grandfathers have a variety of meanings attached to grandparenthood, and reflections of their favorite grandparent when they were children had little association with definitions of grandmotherhood. However, memory of their grandparents have some association with meanings attached to grandfatherhood. Generally, the grandparent-grandchild relationship is valued by older persons.

As Kivnick (1982: 65) noted, grandparenthood "has the potential to provide day-to-day delight and long-term enrichment; it may also be an unrecognized contributor to ongoing unhappiness and bitterness." Families who have had good intergenerational relationships find grandparenting to be a rewarding experience. The older generation can interact with younger family members but they do not have responsibility for them. Grandchildren can learn family history and meanings of family customs from their grandparents. However, if the relationship between the adult children and older generation is tenuous, contact with grandchildren may be minimal. The grandparents may feel unhappy and bitter because they do not have the opportunity to develop relationships with their grandchildren.

Becoming a Grandparent

While there is time for an older person to anticipate the grandparent role, there is not a clearly defined set of expectations for grandparenting. The older person may approach the grandparent-grandchild relationship as if he/she were becoming a parent to a young child again, or he/she may view the grandchild as someone who is to be pampered, leaving the discipline to his/her adult child. Fisher (1983) interviewed 28 grandmothers whose daughters had recently had babies. The findings suggest that there was a great deal of ambiguity about what the grandmothers thought they should do. Some of the grandmothers became emotionally involved with the grandchildren. They valued their grandchildren and seemed to be wrapped up in the relationship. Not surprisingly, they saw themselves as highly involved in the grandparenting role and were glad that they had become grandparents. Other grandmothers emphasized their instrumental involvement. The grandparenting relationship became one of doing things for the grandchild and daughter. Still others stated that becoming a grandmother changed little in their lives.

Fisher analyzed her data in terms of the geographical proximity of the grandmothers to their daughters and found that grandmothers living near their daughters have a less ambiguous definition of what to do when they became grandmothers. The more distant grandmothers have fewer opportunities to develop a relationship with their grandchild and, consequently, may have not experimented with the grandparent role to the same degree.

Most grandparents develop valuable and rewarding relationships with their grandchildren even though they do not have many societal expectations to guide them. Possibly their years of parenthood equipped them for interaction with grandchildren, and the lack of responsibility for the day-to-day care of the child relieves them from some of the burdens. Hence, ambiguity of the grandparent role does not hinder the establishment of a relationship with grandchildren.

Types of Grandparents

With few expectations for grandparenting, it is not surprising that the types of relationships between grandparents and grandchildren vary. The grandparent may develop a very close relationship and share many activities with a grandchild. Or, the grandparent may be very reserved with a grandchild, and their relationship may be characterized by mutual respect. Further, the adult children may influence the way in which a grandchild perceives generational interaction within the family. Although research has not considered the family history of generational interaction, the grandparent-grandchild relationship does not develop in a vacuum. It evolves out of a history of generational interaction among the grandparent, adult child, and grandchild.

In a study of 125 grandmothers living in Madison, Wisconsin, Robertson (1977) and Wood and Robertson (1976) identified four types of grandparents. Of the sample 29 percent were categorized as the *apportioned* grandmothers who were interested in the moral development of their grandchildren and, at the same time, believed that they could indulge them. They did not worry about spoiling their grandchildren.

The *symbolic* type of grandparent wanted to do what was morally right for their grandchildren. They were concerned about their own behavior so that they would present good models to their grandchildren. The symbolic type described 26 percent of the sample.

The third type, *individualized*, was not concerned about the moral development of their grandchildren but, rather, directed attention to their personal relationship with the grandchild. These grandmothers expected their grandchildren to be around when they felt lonely.

The fourth category of grandparents was defined as *remote* and included 28 percent of the sample. A ritualistic, impersonal, and distant type of relationship was developed by the remote grandmothers. The development of a personal relationship with their grandchildren was not an emphasis of these grandmothers.

The four types of grandparent-grandchild relationship described by Robertson were associated with the different lifestyles of the grandparent generation. Grandmothers who were highly involved in activities outside the family (e.g., work, friend, community) were more likely to have a symbolic relationship with their grandchildren. These grandmothers were also younger than grandmothers in the other categories. In contrast, the individualized grandmothers were older and more family oriented. They were less likely to be employed and involved in fewer activities outside the family (e.g., work, community groups, friends). The activity patterns of the apportioned grandmothers were in between those of the symbolic and individualized (i.e., more involved in extrafamily activities than the individualized but less so than the symbolic). Finally, the remote grandmothers seemed to be a unique group of individuals who were generally dissatisfied with their life situation.

Although the grandmothers in Robertson's sample viewed their relationship with their grandchildren differently, nearly 80 percent were happy with their grandparent-grandchild relationship. Most viewed grandparenting as an easier role than parenting and nearly 40 percent enjoyed grandparenting more than parenting. One-quarter stated that they derived equal amounts of enjoyment from grandparenting and parenting. The grandmothers also agreed on the characteristics associated with *good* grandparenting; 80 percent stated that a good grandmother "loves and enjoys grandchildren, sets good examples (religion, honesty, right versus wrong), helps grandchildren when asked or needed, does not interfere too much in grandchildren's lives, is a good listener, doesn't interfere with parental upbringing or spoil grandchildren, and can use discipline with grandchildren if it is needed" (Robertson, 1977: 171).

Grandchildren's Views of Grandparents

Several studies have examined young adults' views of grandparents. Hartshorne and Manaster (1982) questioned 178 young adult grandchildren about the relationship with their grandparents. Generally they had contact and were satisfied with their relationships with the older generation. Grandparents were viewed as important to these grandchildren and they believed that they were important to their grandparents. There was slightly more contact with the maternal grandparents, and the mother's mother was seen as the most important grandparent. Using grandparent categories similar to Robertson, Hartshorne and Manaster found that most of the grandparent-grandchild relationship were either apportioned or remote. This study suggested that the grandparent-grandchild relationship is significant to young adult grandchildren.

Another study of 269 undergraduate women who had living grandparents examined their relationships with their grandparents (Hoffman, 1979-1980). These grandchildren had more contact with their mothers' parents than with their fathers'. Also, they were closer emotionally to their maternal grandparents than their paternal grandparents. Similar to other findings, this study suggested that the grandparent-grandchild relationship is matrilineal.

Robertson (1976) surveyed 86 men and women aged 18 to 26 years concerning the grandparent-grandchild relationship. Developing a personal relationship with grandparents was seen as a positive by these young adults. For example, 92 percent thought that a child would miss something if they did not have a grandparent; 90 percent believed that grandparents were not too old-fashioned to help grandchildren, and 72 percent indicated that grandparents have much influence on a grandchild's life. The primary expectation associated with grandparenthood was the development of an emotional relationship with grandchildren. However, supporting Robertson's (1975) theoretical perspective, the type of relationship and frequency of contact between grandparents and grandchildren were regulated by the parents. Clearly, the parental generation is pivotal.

There is some evidence that the age of the grandchildren may be relevant when considering grandchildren's views of grandparents. Kahana and Kahana (1970) studied 18 grandchildren aged 4 to 5 years, 33 aged 8 to 9 years, and 33 aged 11 to 12 years. On the whole, the grandchildren favorably viewed grandparents and valued their relationships with them. However, the reasons for this positive assessment varied by age group. The youngest age group valued grandparents because they spoiled or indulged them. The middle age group was fond of grandparents because they shared fun or pleasureable activities. The oldest age group seemed to be distant from grandparents and was satisfied with this arrangement. Consequently, it may be important to consider the ages of the grandchildren when focusing the grandparent-grandchild relationship. Given the possibility of health difficulties with grandparents aged 75 years and older, the age of the grandparents may also influence the type of relationship developed with grandchildren.

Divorce and Grandparenting

Since the parental generation mediates relationships between grandchildren and grandparents (Robertson, 1975), changes made by parents are important. For example, if parents are separated or divorced, the grandparent-grandchild relationship may be altered. At least, grandparents may have anxiety because they think this relationship may be in jeopardy. I recall leading a discussion on family relationships with a group of older people living in a nursing home when an elderly woman raised this issue. She asked about divorce among middle-aged adults and then, with personal anxiety, she said, "My daughter and her husband are getting a divorce and I don't know if I will see my grandchildren again." This woman was distressed by the breakup of her daughter's marriage but she was more concerned about the effect it would have on the relationships she had with her grandchildren. The older woman's anxiety should not be surprising nor should it be ignored. The relationship ramifications of divorce are difficult for the parents to assess, and they are more ambiguous for the older generation who may be somewhat removed from the parents' marriage.

A recent study examined the impact of parental divorce on the grandparent-grandchild relationship (Matthews and Sprey, 1984). Eighteen grandparents with at least one divorced child and nineteen with no divorced children were interviewed. While it is important that grandparents know about and are informed of a child's divorce, only 22 percent of the grandparents with divorced children had been informed of the divorce *before* the final decision was made. Of the grandparents 40 percent were surprised by the divorce and 30 percent foresaw it.

Most of the grandparents with no divorced children saw little possibility of a child divorcing but if one should divorce, they expected to be informed *before* it was decided upon by the couple.

The grandparent-grandchild relationship was greatly affected by the assignment of custody of the children. Generally, the wife received custody and the maternal grandparents were able to continue their grandparent relationships. In fact, when their daughters received custody of the grandchildren, all but two of the grandparents reported no change or an increased amount of contact with their grandchildren. Age of the grandchildren was also viewed as relevant because the younger the grandchild, the more likely the divorced parent needs help from the older generation. Similar to Fisher's (1983) findings, Matthews and Sprey found that proximity to grandchildren was crucial because the grandparents living close to their daughters were able to continue an interaction pattern more easily.

The finding that contact between grandparents and grandchildren is influenced by which parent receives custody of the children under-scores the feelings of anxiety expressed by grandparents. The child's divorce may hinder contact with grandchildren. A review of the legal rights of grandparents indicated that grandparents have minimal legal standing (Wilson and DeShane, 1982). To remedy the lack of grandparents' legal standing when a parent divorces, Oregon passed a law in 1979 that recognized grandparents' rights. This law permitted the petitioning of visitation rights by grandparents.

Without a doubt, grandparents' legal situation is ambiguous in the United States. Wilson and DeShane (1982) linked the legal ambiguity to the confusion with the cultural definition of grandparent. They suggested that

> it is naive to expect grandparents to be awarded explicit legal standing given the cultural ambiguity of the grandparent role in the United States. The limited research that has addressed the culture position of grandparents has largely affirmed the ambiguous position of America's grandparents. Whether we can expect legislative mandate to resolve the issue is debatable.

Future Research Needs on Grandparenting

The research on grandparenting suggests that grandparenthood is valued by the older and younger generations. The middle generation is the mediator of the relationship between grandparents and grandchildren, and most of the grandparent lineage is maternal. There are few expectations associated with grandparenting, and several different types of grandparenting have been identified. One concern of grandparents is the affect of a child's divorce on the relationship with their grandchildren. Legal rights of grandparents have been advanced by an Oregon law but ambiguity continues. Generally, the grandparent-grandchild relationship is a positive, rewarding experience for both generations.

The grandfather-grandchild relationship needs to be explored. While there are a number of studies on grandmothering, there is little known about grandfatherhood. Is the grandfather-grandson relationship similar to the grandfather-granddaughter relationship? Are grandfathers as involved in grandparenting as grandmothers? Do grandchildren view grandfathers differently than they do grandmothers? There are a number of questions about grandfatherhood that have not been examined.

Most of the grandparent research has been descriptive, and there is a need for analytical studies in this area. There are a number of factors that may influence the grandparent-grandchild relationship that have not been included in the research. For example, ethnic background might influence the interactions between the generations (Woehrer, 1978). Another factor is social class. Clavan (1978) theorized that differences between the middle and lower socioeconomic classes may affect the degree to which grandparents are seen as central to the family. Race is a third factor that has been neglected in grandparenting studies. Research on grandparenthood needs to move beyond the description of types of grandparenting to consider the many factors that might influence the grandparent-grandchild relationship.

While the effect of a child's divorce on the grandparent-grandchild relationship has been the focus of a few studies, this area needs more research. Possibly, some of the ambiguity surrounding grandparents' legal rights can be removed by research on the positive aspects of the grandparent-grandchild relationship in divorced, single parent families.

Grandparents are a vital part of later life families and their interaction is based on a many years of a parent-child relationship. With the middle generation as mediators, the importance of past interactions between the older and middle generations cannot be underestimated. Therefore, grandparent research needs to include the family history of interaction. When the older and middle generations have strained relationships, what type of grandparent-grandchild relationship develops? How do these grandchildren view their grandparents? In other words, how does the affective relationship between the middle and older generations influence the relationship between the older and younger generations? The history of family interaction is an important variable.

THE SIBLING RELATIONSHIP

Society's emphasis on the nuclear family has focused attention on the marital, adult child, and grandparent relationships in later life and has neglected the sibling relationship. Recently, research has been directed toward the interaction with siblings in later life. In terms of family relationships, siblings are important to older people. The unmarried childless elderly rely on their siblings to provide assistance. Often, older brothers and sisters provide emotional support to one another when they experience a loss in later life. Sometimes, elderly brothers and sisters reside together in their later years. While many individuals have siblings throughout their lives, the number of siblings declines with age. However, most older people have at least one living sibling. Research indicated that between 75 percent and more than 90 percent of older persons have at least one living brother or sister (Scott, 1983; Cicirelli, 1980, Harris et al., 1975). The sibling relationship is an important relationship to older people and its viability for potential support in later life should not be overlooked.

Uniqueness of the Sibling Relationship

Sibling relationships are different from other family relationships in at least four ways (Cicirelli, 1982). First, the sibling relationship has the potential for being the longest family relationshp. It begins at birth and ends with the death of one of the siblings. Marriage begins many years after birth. Parenthood begins with birth but generally the parents precede their offspring into death by several years. Usually, siblings' births and deaths are within a few years of each other. Therefore, there is a potential for a long duration of this family relationship. The second unique characteristic is that siblings share a common heritage, environment, and childhood. Their perspectives on family life and cultural expectations have been developed within the same cultural milieu.

Thus it is not uncommon for siblings to share experiences and perspectives that their own spouses of many years do not understand. The common heritage encourages siblings to discuss childhood events that occurred fifty years ago.

Third, Cicirelli (1982) suggests that the sibling relationship are highly egalitarian. The siblings do not have any prescribed power over one another as found in the parent-child relationship. Theoretically, they hold relatively equal power in the relationship. The fourth unique feature of the sibling relationship is that it is an ascribed rather than earned role. A person is born into a family with siblings, and achievements do not alter the ascribed natured of the sibling relationship.

While siblings may live far apart and seldom see each other, the potential duration of the relationship, common heritage, egalitarian nature, and ascribed role contribute to make the sibling relationship unique. Childhood experiences bind the individuals together in a manner uncommon to other social relationships. Consequently, the historical nature of sibling interaction is important. Childhood experiences may draw older siblings together or, in some cases, they may hinder later life interaction. The sibling relationship in later life provides an opportunity to explore a family relationship which has several unique characteristics.

Contact Between Older Siblings

Several studies have examined the amount of contact between older brothers and sisters. Recently, Scott (1983) analyzed data from a sample of 199 older men and women. Most of these persons had living siblings and contact was most frequent with those who lived within 31 to 60 minutes. Contact by telephone was more frequent than by letter. For example, approximately one-half had at least weekly telephone contact with a sibling. Only one in ten did not have contact with a sibling by telephone while two-thirds never corresponded with their siblings. These data suggested that the sibling relationship is most frequently maintained by face-to-face contacts and telephone conversations. Written communication is a relatively infrequent form of interaction for older siblings.

Cicirelli (1980) found that 17 percent of the his sample of older persons saw their siblings weekly while another 33 percent visited with them at least once a month; 56 percent had face-to-face contact with their siblings several time a year. He also found that 26 percent of the siblings who had the most contact resided in the same city and 56 percent within 100 miles of each other. Other studies found similar patterns. After reviewing the research on sibling interaction Cicirelli (1982: 272) concluded that "most siblings continue to have contact with each other at least several times a year . . . through their adult years into old age. There is some evidence that contact with siblings declines with advancing age . . . but contact ceases entirely for very few."

As a person matures into adulthood, contact with siblings becomes less frequent. Brothers and sisters marry and focus attention on their own expanding families and lifestyles. Over the years it is likely that they continue the sibling relationship with minimized contact but seldom sever the relationship. In the later years, there is no indication that the pattern of interaction established throughout their lives is altered.

Siblings' Feelings of Closeness

Brothers' and sisters' feelings of closeness developed while they frequently interacted in childhood. In later life, the frequency of interaction declines but their feelings of closeness may continue. Ross and Milgram (1982) interviewed a sample of 75 siblings including 22 who were aged 70 to 93 years. The older siblings had a stronger sense of family unity than younger siblings in the same sample—few older brothers or sisters stated that they never felt close to their siblings. The older siblings saw their brothers or sisters as friends or confidants more often than the younger group. Feelings of closeness seldom developed after the brothers and sisters reached adulthood. Childhood provided the frequent interaction and shared experience that fostered feelings of closeness and these feelings continued into later life even though the contact decreased. Memories of shared experiences acted as bonds to draw the siblings together.

Another study of closeness suggested that the sibling nearest in age to the respondent was usually the seen as closest brother or sister (Adams, 1968). Cicirelli (1982; 1980) found that feelings of closeness among older siblings is related to the amount of contact they have had with each other. In contrast, Allan (1977) found that older brothers and sisters felt involved with each other even though they had not had much contact with one another. Similar to the Ross and Milgram (1982) study, Allen's data suggested that the sibling relationship is cemented in the younger years and continues to be important even though contact is diminished.

Gender Differences Between Siblings

Gender may be related to differences in sibling relationships. Feeling of affection have been found to be stronger between sisters when compared to brothers (Adams, 1968). Further, adult brothers are more competitive and jealous than sisters. Sisters are more influential than brothers. Also, sisters appear to be emotionally supportive of brothers as they age and experience changes in later life. For women, their sisters appear to challenge them to maintain their social roles in later life. In some ways, sisters also are competitive with one another (Cicirelli, 1977). However, Scott (1983) did not find any differences in the amount of contact or affectional ties on the basis of gender.

Although the research is not conclusive, there is some evidence that gender differences may influence the sibling relationship. Research on the early development of sibling relationships points toward the possibility of closer relationships between same-gender siblings than between opposite-gender siblings. Further, sisters appear to have the closest relationships. Additional research is needed to determine if these gender differences continue into later life family patterns. There is a need for longitudinal studies to ascertain if siblings continue or alter their feelings of affection as they grow older.

Death of a Sibling

There is a paucity of research focusing on the effect of the death of a sibling in later life. When a sibling dies, surviving brothers and sisters are reminded of their own mortality. If the deceased sibling is the first brother or sister to die, the feelings may be intensified. The author recalls the death of the first sibling in a family, and the grief associated the death appeared to be heightened because this sibling was the third in a line of six brothers and sisters. The transitory nature of life was illustrated to the survivors. They remarked that the person was "not very old" because she was "not the oldest in the family."

Whenever a family experiences the loss of a member, feelings of grief characterize the survivors. Siblings provide assistance to deal with the initial adjustment to the loss. If the deceased sibling is younger, do they reassess their own lives? Is the grieving process exacerbated because they are dealing with the loss *and* with concerns about their own deaths? Later life families experience the deaths of siblings at various ages and little is known about the impact of siblings' deaths.

Importance of Sibling Relationships

Sibling relationships are important to older persons. It is a family relationship that endures throughout life even though interaction may diminish with age. Although adult children provide more assistance to older parents, older siblings help one another and are supportive of each other. Given the resiliency of the sibling relationship, future research should identify factors that strengthen older brother and sister relationships. Siblings may provide mutual support if both are widowed. There is no doubt that siblings are significant in the lives of many older people.

OTHER FAMILY RELATIONSHIPS

Other family relationships may provide emotional and other types of support to later life family members. For example, the childless elderly develop relationships with nieces and nephews as the younger generation matures. As adults, the nieces and nephews continue this relationship with their elderly family members. At the time of a family member's death, various kin provide emotional support to the survivor. Cousins, nieces, nephews, and other kin may attend the funeral or write to encourage the survivor during this difficult time. Although there are situations in which other kin have relationships with older family members, little research has focused on this topic. How important are the other kin to older family members? Do older family members turn to other kin for assistance? Our research efforts have focused on the primacy of the nuclear family and this has limited our knowledge about the vitality of the extended family.

Since there is evidence that the extended family, while modified, has been active as a support network to individuals throughout their lives, there is no reason for it to neglect its members in later life. In fact, the extended family may become more active in later life because the contracting size may encourage kinship interaction (Hess and Waring,

1978). Future research will, one hopes, view later life families as extended families.

Another group of other relatives includes individuals who are not legally members of the kinship network but who are defined as kin by the older person. Herr and Weakland (1979) have labeled this group as the "non-blood-related kin" and Sussman (1976) used the term "fictive kin." These persons are just as important, and in some instances more important, to the later life family member as legally defined relatives. The older person's definition of family includes these individuals, and they expect to maintain a relationship with them. Herr and Weakland (1979: 128) stated that these persons are "the most frequent candidates to be overlooked in a family system by the counselor." There are several types of individuals who might be considered fictive kin. For example, the older person may have interacted with and become a confidant to a younger person over the years. As the relationship developed, the older person may have treated this person "as if he/she were family." Another category may be neighbors with whom the older person is very intimate. These persons may be considered family members on the basis of the older person's definition of family; thus the older person should be asked if there are any non-blood relatives. However, little is known about fictive kin in later life.

SUMMARY

Grandparenthood is a life situation that characterizes many later life families; grandparents are the links between the older and younger generations within a family. Although societal expectations associated with grandparenting are ambiguous, research has demonstrated that grandparents value grandchildren and grandchildren feel positive toward grandparents. Parents are mediators of the grandparent-grandchild relationship. Consequently, parental divorce may influence the relationship between grandparents and grandchildren. Descriptive research has been completed on grandparenting while there is a need for analytical studies in this area.

Older people interact with and value their sibling relationships. The common heritage and childhood experiences are the bonds that hold the sibling relationship together for many years. It is a unique family relationship that should not be overlooked in later life families. It is typical for siblings to decrease the amount of contact over the years.

However, in later life they continue minimal interaction and value the relationship. For some, contact is increased in later life.

Fictive kin are another group that is generally neglected in the later life family research. However, there are individuals older people define as family members and expect them to behave like family. These persons are not blood related and are usually overlooked by service providers and researchers. More attention needs to be directed toward the fictive kin because they represent a viable support system to some older people.

REVIEW QUESTIONS

(1) What is the value of grandparenting to the older adult and younger generations?

(2) How do you describe the various types of grandparent-grandchild relationships?

(3) How does divorce of an adult child affect the grandparent-grandchild relationship?

(4) What is the importance of sibling relationships to older people?

(5) What are the other kin relationships an older person might have, and what is the importance of these relationships to older people?

SUGGESTED PROJECTS

(1) Interview your grandparents and ask them about the importance of the grandparenting role. Ask your parents and siblings about the ways they define the grandparents. Can you identify different types of grandparenting styles?

(2) Talk with your brothers and sisters about what how they think you will interact when you get older. Discuss the relevancy of the sibling relationship with your parents.

CHAPTER
5

Widowhood

When the man to whom you have been married for more than thirty
years dies, a piece of you that you will never know again goes out the door
with him. . . . Thirty years of being us was suddenly transformed into just
me. . . . The end of a marriage [Mooney, 1981: 12, 13].

For many, especially older women, the culmination of marriage is
marked by a transition into widowhood. There are more than 7.5 million
widows and 1.2 million widowers aged 65 years and older in our society
(U. S. Department of Commerce, 1983). Another 2 million women aged
55 to 64 years are widowed and approximately 355,000 men aged 55 to
64 years have experienced the death of a spouse. Widowhood is one
major characteristic of family relationships in later life. Since women
tend to marry men a few years older than themselves and men tend to
live approximately seven fewer years than women, it is not surprising
that there are more widows than widowers. Although widowhood
signifies the end of a marriage, it does not conclude family interaction. In
fact, a marriage may have ended in the temporal sense but it continues
in the minds of the survivors. Survivors' daily activities and decisions
continue to be influenced by the previous marital and family relationships.

In this chapter, research on widowhood will be reviewed. Since
widowhood is primarily a female phenomenon, research has focused on
widows more than widowers. However, male survivorship will be
discussed. The following questions will be addressed: What are the
different situations in which an older person becomes widowed, and
how do the differences relate to adjustment to widowhood? How do
widowed, older individuals respond during the few months after the
death of a spouse? What characterizes the lifestyle of a widowed, older
person? What are the differences between older female and male
survivorship?

DIVERSE PATHS TO WIDOWHOOD

Becoming widowed is a process and an event that differs for many
people, and it is a role for which there is little prior training on what to do
and what not to do. Further, there is little positive anticipation
associated with becoming a widow. The end of marriage and the
beginning of widowhood occur in several different ways. First, a spouse

may suddenly and unexpectedly become widowed. There may be little indication that the husband or wife is going to die, and the death abruptly concludes the marital relationship that had been established many years ago. An example is when a person who has been in reasonably good health suffers a massive heart attack at work. The individual may have been in his/her late fifties or early sixties and planning for retirement with his/her spouse. There was no opportunity for the survivor to anticipate the loss of his/her mate—actually, the survivor was expecting to enjoy retirement years with his/her spouse.

In a recent study of 505 widowed, older persons in England, 4 percent were suddenly widowed (Bowling and Cartwright, 1982). The small portion of suddenly widowed was also found in a study of widows living in Chicago (Lopata, 1973). Although this group of widows was small, they were unique because they had little forewarning that they might be without their spouses, and their lives were radically changed.

For the second type of widow, the death of a spouse was expected and signified the end of a struggle with health problems which had changed the couple's life. The illness may have been the focal point of the couple's life for several years. The death is the final release from the pain and suffering experienced by the deceased as well as the survivor. Approximately 50 percent of the Chicago widows cared for their husbands prior to their deaths (Lopata, 1973). In fact, 40 percent cared for their husbands for more than a year. For example, one widow stated that her husband had been sick for eleven years and was bedridden for seven of those years. In the British study, the expected death was most characteristic of the survivors aged 85 years and older (Bowling and Cartwright, 1982). Generally, the deceased had cancer, or possibly a stroke, that interfered with daily activities and changed the lives of both spouses. For many, the survivors cared for the deceased at home for many years, and toward the end, the care shifted to a hospital. With the move to the hospital, the surviving spouse reorganized life around the dependent mate in an institutional setting.

Concommitant with the loss of a spouse, the survivor who expected the death is relieved of the caregiving responsibilities and discovers that the caregiving lifestyle is no longer needed. In many ways, the expected death may be more difficult than the sudden because the survivor has reorganized his/her life around a dependent person. The daily tasks of caregiving, visits to the doctor or hospital, and other daily routines associated with caregiving are no longer necessary. Consequently, the survivor needs to cope with feelings of loss of spouse and caregiver role as well as a feeling of relief.

The third group is similar to the second in that their spouses were ill prior to death, but they did not expect the deaths. The deceased spouse's illness was not seen as life threatening, or the couple was not informed about the severity of the health condition. More than half the British sample were in this category. One widow stated that her husband had back problems for nine years and died of an unexpected heart attack. He also had cancer, but none of the doctors had informed them of this problem. For this group of widows, the illness did not lead to a complete reorganization of their lives around caregiving. They lived life with their mates in a somewhat restricted manner because of the health problem, but it was something with which they coped and death was not seen as being eminent. Their plans as a couple may have been limited as a result of the illness, but they anticipated life together in the future. Consequently, the marital situation before the death differs from that of the sudden or expected widows.

Becoming a widow is a process that may begin, albeit reluctantly, before the event occurs. Or it may arrive with no anticipation of what it is like to be without one's spouse. For example, the quote at the beginning of this chapter was written by a widow whose husband died suddenly. Being widowed was not expected nor was it considered. Consequently, she began widowhood without any preparation. For both men and women, the marital experiences and situations prior to the death of a spouse are significant factors to consider when examining the adjustment to being without a spouse.

THE FIRST FEW MONTHS OF WIDOWHOOD

Similar to any role change, the initial time period of widowhood represents the severing of a former relationship and the beginning of a new set of expectations and relationships. Unlike many other roles, becoming a widow is unique. First, to become a widow one must have been married. Marriage is a very intimate and extraordinary human relationship. For the older widowed, the marriage may have endured for a long time and widowhood represents a radical change in their lives. Second, widowhood is not welcomed. Most people want marriage to continue and few wish death to occur. For example, a couple experiences role changes when they marry but the changes are welcomed and encouraged. A third unique feature is that the loss is irreplaceable and widowhood cannot be avoided. Even if the surviving spouse remarries, the memory of the former mate continues—the family history generated by the initial marriage is not expunged. As a result of the uniqueness of the widowhood role, the first few months are important.

Grief is one of the initial feelings a widow experiences. Research suggests that individuals differ in the ways they grieve about the loss of spouse (Parkes, 1972). However, there are several stages that characterize most persons' grieving process. During the first few days, weeks, and, for some, months the survivor is in a state of chaos. The person may feel anger at the loss of the spouse ("Why did he/she abandon me?"), disbelief ("I can't believe this is happening to me.") and confusion about the future ("What am I going to do now?"). This stage has been called the "crisis-loss-phase" (Bankoff, 1983). The survivor's response is related to the disorganization in the person's social life that is caused by the spouse's death. Moving from a spouse role to a widowed role in a short time period creates a great deal of confusion as to what to do and what the future holds for the survivor. This is exacerbated by the emotional attachments the bereaved has for the deceased. Widowed individuals have two major tasks thrust upon them: They need to mourn the loss of a loved one *and* form a new life.

In the crisis-loss-phase, the survivor may become apathetic and seek to withdraw from the social relationships established by the couple. Feelings of abandonment and being single discourage many of the existing social relationships. Consequently, the widowed may ignore reality and seek to postpone decisions and interactions they perceive as painful. This is a time when grief becomes the focus of the person, and they have difficulty dealing with day-to-day activities.

The second stage, the "transition-phase," is when the survivor attempts to create a new life (Bankoff, 1983). Grief, while still a feeling, has lessened in its intensity and the survivor begins to recognize that there is a new life that can be established. Relationships can be renegotiated or created without the presence of a spouse. The individual begins to look beyond the loss of a mate to the alternatives for themselves. In this stage, the development of a new identity becomes a major task. This identity centers around the need to see oneself as a single rather than a married person. Sociologically, the survivor in the transition phase is beginning to rebuild a social system that became disorganized as a result of the spouse's death.

The final stage entails the establishment and continuation of a new lifestyle. The reorganization may result in a new life as a single, widowed person particularly if the wife survived. Or, as in the case of many widowers, a remarriage may occur. This is the stage during which life returns to normal and the grief is minimal. The widowed person has a new identity and can realistically no longer rely on the former marriage for self-definition. This, however, does not mean that the survivor forgets about the former marriage; rather, he/she adjusts to the loss.

Since our society has no definition of an appropriate amount of time for grieving, it is not surprising that the time each widowed person spends in the stages vary. Based on her study of urban widows, Lopata (1973) suggested that the intensity of the grief feelings begins to decline after about six weeks and is minimal after six months. However, she also found that around 20 percent stated that they have never gotten over the death of their husbands. The grief is something they must always deal with. Researchers have found that some survivors have difficulty dealing with their feelings of grief and do not want to discuss them, even though the death occurred several months before the interview (Bowling and Cartwright, 1982). While the length of the grieving process varies, most survivors have worked through their intense feelings within six months and are beginning to reorganize their lives. At the same time, this author suggests that it is difficult to ever get over the loss of a spouse, especially when the survivor spent many years in a marital relationship bonded by affection, interaction, and experiences.

In an attempt to identify the problems experienced soon after the death of a spouse, Helena Lopata (1979) asked widows to list the main problems they faced immediately following their husbands' deaths. Most frequently mentioned difficulties were practical issues related to the funeral arrangements and financial matters. The next frequent problem was dealing with emotions, the strongest of which were their feelings of loneliness and loss. The interrelatedness of the practical and emotional problems cannot be overlooked and may contribute to the chaotic nature of the crisis stage. Also, Lopata (1979) found that one-sixth of her sample did not identify any problems right after the death of their spouses. It may be that these persons were attempting to ignore or deny the crisis they experienced after their spouses died.

The first few months of widowhood are difficult, and the survivor's ability to deal with crisis is important. Losing a spouse creates a vacuum in one's social network, and the filling of this void takes time and support from others. The problems entail everyday tasks as well as emotions developed over a long time of togetherness. Even if the marriage was not a strong one, the death creates disorganization. While the survivor is faced with his/her own problems, there are difficulties associated with others who also feel loss. In many instances, the death of a husband is also the death of a father, and the children's grief is recognized by the surviving spouse. The family as a whole is altered by the death, and the widowed person may become the focal point for the reorganization of the family.

For a few, the reorganization of the family involves moving into another house shortly after the death (Bowling and Cartwright, 1982). In the British study, 5 percent moved to a new residence after they became widowed. Nearly half the movers formed multigenerational households. Some of these stated that their families encouraged them to move in with them. However, satisfaction with the move varied. Most stated that they were glad they moved so soon after they became widowed, and some regretted the move. Given the characteristics of the grief process, the timing of the decision to move is important. If a widowed person is in the crisis stage and has intense feelings of grief, the move may be problematic. However, if the person is in the transition stage, the move may be a realistic way to reorganize one's life.

Sanctification of the husband is one process that widows have employed to help with the difficulties of widowhood (Lopata, 1981; 1979). This involves viewing the deceased husband as sacred—the deceased person is above reproach and flawless. Lopata (1979) stated that sanctification functions to help the survivor work through grief and bolster his/her own self-esteem. Having been married to a "flawless" person may lift a person's morale lowered by the loss of spouse. For whatever reasons, widows tended to idealize their deceased spouses as being "unusually good husbands," "very good fathers," and stated that their husbands "had no irritating habits." Lopata (1979: 141) summarized the sanctification process as follows:

> The late husband is seen as . . . an ideal type of man. Such sanctification performs many functions which provide comfort, a sense of having been

important to an important man. . . . Sanctification evolves the widow out of the double bind of having to mourn the late husband while simultaneously reestablishing herself as a partnerless person and rebuilding her support systems without him. Purified of mortal jealousies and other feelings, he is seen as a benevolent saint, blessing her efforts at a full life without him.

While most widows tend to sanctify their husbands, there are differences by age and education (Lopata, 1981). Minority and less educated women idealized their husbands less than did white and more highly educated women. Also, the older, white widows were more likely to sanctify their husbands than the younger, black survivors. Although there was some idealization of the deceased husband, Lopata (1981) noted that some of the least educated expressed hostility and dissatisfaction about the former relationship with their husbands.

The sanctification process may be related to the widow's recollection of the former marriage. This idealization of the husband is an interesting phenomenon and influences the reorganization of a widowed person's life. For example, as noted in Chapter 2, the remarriage of a widowed person may be complicated by the idealization of the former spouse.

WIDOWHOOD AS A WAY OF LIFE

Immediately following the death of a spouse, the family rallies around the survivor. Children, siblings, and other relatives contact the widowed person to provide emotional support and help with many day-to-day activities. In addition, friends and neighbors join these kin in their sorrow and grief associated with the death. For example, neighbors may prepare meals for the family before and after the funeral or share their houses with out-of-town guests. The most immediate response to the death is activation of the survivor's social network so that he/she is freed from the daily routines and has some time to deal with grief.

As the time progresses, the social network decreases its support of the widowed person. The neighbors and friends may look after the survivor or help with special projects (e.g., mow the lawn), but there is an expectation that the survivor is responsible for day-to-day activities. Children and siblings may continue their support; however, it decreases a few weeks after the funeral. Generally, the social network is on alert but not on active duty several weeks after the death.

The studies (Lopata, 1979; 1973) of Chicago widows indicated that children provided help by caring for the ill prior to their death, assisting with the funeral arrangements, providing emotional support, and completing various household tasks. For most, children were involved in the support of the survivor prior to the death as well as after.

Widows received more help from daughters and daughters-in-law than from sons and sons-in-law (Lopata, 1979; 1973). There is a special relationship between the mothers and daughters in dealing with widowhood. Compared to male offspring, female offspring were more likely to provide support to the survivor throughout an illness as well as after the death. The relationship is also unique because the daughters are most likely to provide emotional support when the widow feels depressed. For some, the daughter becomes a confidant who provides comfort for the widow. The sons are expected to give advice and task-oriented support, but not necessarily emotional support.

The gender differences in the types of support provided are related to the gender definitions of men and women within family networks. For many persons, women are viewed as emotional reservoirs who can encourage those who are depressed. The men are responsible for various tasks (such as financial planning, making household repairs). As definitions of masculinity and femininity change, older widows' expectations of their daughters and sons may change. Men may be expected to provide more emotional support while daughters may be requested to provide suggestions on financial and other issues. However, the current research on widows indicates that there are gender differentiations as to what types of support widows expect from the male and female offspring.

A latent function of the close tie between the widows and female offspring may be the opportunity for anticipatory socialization for younger generations. With the gender gap in longevity rates, many daughters and daughters-in-law are likely to become widowed. Daughters of widows are in the position to learn about the problems and adjustment difficulties associated with widowhood.

The widowed person's response to the help provided by the support network may vary depending on the widow's stage of grief. In the crisis stage, the survivor has withdrawn from reality. The assistance provided by children and others in the support network may have little impact on the survivor. Later, after the intense grief subsides, the survivor may be more receptive to help from others. A study of 98 women widowed 18 months or less and 147 women widowed 19 to 35 months examined the effects of support networks (Bankoff, 1983). The primary concern was the psychological well-being of the widows. The findings suggested that the stage of grief influences the impact of the support provided by the social network. For the widows in the crisis stage, overall support did not influence feelings of well-being. In the transition stage, the more the network provided support, the higher the well-being of the survivor. Various types of support including contact, intimacy, emergency assistance, emotional guidance, and approval of new lifestyle were examined. Only one form of support, emotional, had any positive effect on the newly bereaved widows' well-being. Transitional widows' feelings of well-being were influenced by three types of support (i.e., contact, intimacy, and emotional).

The source of support was especially important to the crisis stage widows. Widows' parents were the most influential supporters and other widowed persons were the next most important sources of support for these widows. In contrast, the source of the support had little effect on the widows in the transition stage. This study suggests that the mobilization of the support network is important to widows, but their ability to receive its benefits is mediated by the closeness to the death. Widows in the crisis stage are focusing on feelings of grief and have difficulty recognizing available resources as well as the importance of these resources.

Building on Lopata's (1979) examination of the social supports of women in Chicago, Gloria Heinemann (1983) focused on the strength of the widows' support networks. Reciprocity was defined as the basis of the family support network and the primary emphasis was on relationships with various family members and friends. Generally, the findings indicated that the widows with strong family ties did not necessarily have positive attitudes or attractive dispositions. Widows with the most problems and difficulties tended to have the stronger family support networks. Apparently, the more vulnerable and dependent widows received support from family; although the family's support of the dependent widow may be premised on reciprocity, the family becomes tolerant of the older widow's feelings of hostility and dissatisfaction with life.

For many widowed persons, the first few months after the death of a spouse is a time of adjustment to living alone. It is likely that they have shared a household with the spouse for many years, and now they are in a situation in which they are the only one in the home. Half the widowed individuals who lived alone in the British study stated that loneliness was a big problem (Bowling and Cartwright, 1982). Approximately two-thirds of these widowed persons found it "very difficult" or "fairly difficult" to adjust to living alone. Another third stated that it was not a difficult adjustment. Difficulties centered on the emotional and psychological voids in not having someone with whom to talk and share things with as well as on problems relating to day-to-day living. The day-to-day problems included financial concerns, size of house, and getting household tasks done. These data suggest that living alone is a problem, and widowed persons feel isolated because of it. Consequently, one of the tasks a widowed person needs to address is the reorganization of life as one person in the house.

While most widowed individuals report these problems, some have little difficulty making adjustments. However, research does not provide insight as to why some have fewer difficulties—it might be that their marriage was characterized by little sharing and companionship and, although the loss of a spouse is traumatic, their adjustment to the day-to-day living situation is minimal. Another plausible explanation is that these widowed persons may have been close to another widowed person and had some insights as to what to expect after their spouse died. With the current research, these explanations are only hypotheses.

Widows' tendency to withdraw from social relationships and frequent reports of living alone suggest that the bereaved are isolated (Bowling and Cartwright, 1982). A recent study of 75 older widows and 57 married older women examined social isolation (Anderson, 1984). In contrast to myths about isolation, these widows had more primary relationships than the married women. The married and widowed women reported strong relationships with children but the widowed had more close relationships with siblings and other relatives. The loss of spouse enhanced the development of relationships beyond the widow's nuclear family. There was some difference in who was considered for certain needs. For emotional concerns and worries, the widows turned to their children. However, if they were ill or needed financial assistance they were more likely to turn to siblings. This study suggests that the widows are not isolated from family support networks and, after the death of their husbands, they tend to build intimate ties with siblings and other relatives.

Widowed individuals who have been widowed for one to two years exhibit reorganized lifestyles. They have developed ways to cope with the day-to-day problems of living alone and receive emotional support from various persons. Their support networks include various relatives, especially children and siblings, and former or new friends. While there are feelings of loneliness and a sense of loss, these widows have developed ways to cope with these problems. These survivors have established a new identity with the help of their support network.

Analysis of data from a national sample presented evidence that the widowed have a viable informal support group (Kohen, 1983). The study included 40 widowers, 226 widows, 217 married men, and 158 married women who were aged 55 years or older. It was found that the widowed had more contact with relatives, friends, and neighbors than did the married persons. Apparently the married persons focused on their couple relationship while the widowed, who were alone, cultivated their relationships with others. These data also suggested that the women, married or widowed, had a more extensive social network than the married or widowed men.

For some widowed persons, employment may become more important after the death of a spouse. Possibly, the widowed person has been employed and concentrates more energy on the job after the death. However, it is unrealistic to expect widows to substitute employment for marriage. Morgan (1980) illustrated that few widows who have not been employed become so after they are widowed. Further, employed widows do not increase the number of hours they spend on the job. Future groups of widows may be more oriented toward work and employment may be elevated after they become widowed. But, at this time, employment is not elevated after women become widowed.

One study examined the living situations of rural, Black widowed persons as compared to a random sample of rural older persons (Scott and Kivett, 1980). The findings indicated that Black survivors who live in a rural environment may be particularly isolated and in need of formal supports to deal with the long-term effects of widowhood. Compared to other rural persons, the Black, widowed individuals were more likely to be isolated, have inadequate incomes, and be in poor health. Transportation was also a problem for this group. Further, they were less aware of available services to help them meet their needs. Scott and Kivett (1980) suggested that social policies do not recognize the particularly disadvantaged position of the Black, rural widowed. While the rural widowed may be particularly vulnerable, the lack of reliance on formal support networks has also been found in the urban setting. For example, Lopata (1979) reported that urban widows do not rely on the array of resources available to them. Adjustment to widowhood as a way of life may be enhanced by targeted services to the most disadvantaged widowed persons in both the rural and urban settings.

While support from family, friends, and other relatives as well as help provided by formal social service agencies are important to the long-term adjustment of widowed persons, the development of a reorganized, independent lifestyle is desired (Silverstone and Hyman, 1982). Persons providing support need to recognize the survivor's stage in the grieving process and provide support that will encourage the long-term adjustment to the loss. After the mourning and grief have been minimized, the survivors need to be given the opportunity to experiment with who they are and how they want to reestablish their lives. Encouragement for the development of an independent lifestyle buttressed with the informal and formal support networks contributes to the establishment of a new identity for the widowed persons and overall long-term adjustment to widowhood.

WIDOWHOOD VERSUS WIDOWERHOOD

Differences between male and female adjustments to widowhood have been examined. Do adjustment patterns of men and women survivors differ after the death of their spouses? Do widows fare better than widowers? Within recent years a number of studies have focused on both husbands and wives who have suffered the loss of a spouse. In 1970, Felix Berardo published an article that suggested widowers are more isolated than widows. Also, widowers had difficulty with the completion of many household tasks because their wives had been responsible for them. Consequently, loss of a spouse may contribute to social isolation for widowers and adjustment may be more difficult for men than for women survivors. Theoretically, if the female is the primary liaison for social relationships, her death has the potential of severing many of the husband's social relationships. Also, if the couple has a traditional division of household activities, the wife is probably responsible for many of the domestic tasks. Her death may force the husband to learn how to accomplish many of these tasks. For some men, this might be the first time they have had this responsibility. Therefore, they need to deal with emotional as well as instrumental losses as a result of their spouses' death.

The social relationships of widows, widowers, and married couples have been compared in a study of older persons living in two upper-middle-class retirement communities (Longino and Lipman, 1981). The older women, both married and widowed, had more extensive social contacts than the men. Widowers had the fewest primary relationships. The authors suggested that the energy women spent on developing relationships with family and other persons during their younger years appears to pay off in later life. Women may be spouseless but they were not without their family and friendship ties. Widowers had frequent contact with individuals who provided services to them. In fact, men were more likely to receive instrumental support and women usually received emotional support.

Another analysis of the social involvement of male and female survivors was based on data from a national sample (Hyman, 1983). Similar to other studies, widows were found to have increased social contacts with their informal social network. However, widowers' interaction patterns revealed no such pattern. Widowed men continued interacting with individuals with whom they had relationships before their spouses died. Moreover, neither the female nor male widowed changed their involvement in religious activities after the death of their spouses. These data suggest that widowers continue their interaction patterns into widowhood while widows increase their informal social contacts.

Similar to other studies, an analysis of the Louis Harris survey data found that the widowed had slightly lower social participation than married persons (Arens, 1982-1983). Also, widowers spent less time with friends than widows. However, widowhood did not appear to be the reason for limited social involvement. Arens concluded that the widowed persons were older, more unhealthy, and less educated than the married persons. Further, widows experienced more serious financial difficulties. It may be that the widowed individuals are as gregarious as married persons and factors other than the loss of spouse restrict their social interaction. For most survivors, involvement with other people is probably related to the amount of social interaction they previously had. If they had a vibrant, extensive social circle with their spouses, they are likely to be socially involved during widowhood. If they tended to limit their social contacts before their spouses died, they are likely to be homebodies as widowed persons.

Even though widows have more social contacts than widowers, there is some evidence that female survivors have more emotional problems adjusting to the death of spouse (Bowling and Cartwright, 1982). Both widows and widowers reported similar feelings of loneliness in this study. The differences in the emotional adjustments of male and female survivors is intriguing because the widows received more support for their emotional responses. As Bowling and Cartwright (1982: 148) suggested, the "widows were either finding it more difficult to adjust emotionally to their new role, or they were more prepared to recognize and talk about the difficulty." Possibly, frequent emotional support encouraged widows to express emotional concerns about their *own* adjustment to widowhood.

In the British study of widowhood, men and women were queried about their involvement in domestic activities (Bowling and Cartwright, 1982). Both male and female survivors were likely to have started doing their former spouses' household tasks before the death. Generally the couples had traditional divisions of household responsibility. However, following the death of a spouse, the men were cooking, washing clothes, making beds and shopping whereas the women were gardening and doing odd jobs around the house. Most of the widowed persons stated that they either liked or were ambivalent about the new tasks they had thrust upon them. When dissatisfaction was expressed, it was from the widowers who were more likely to be unhappy with the changes than were the widows. Middle-class widows were more likely to have paid help than middle-class widowers. Although there are differences in the type of domestic activities performed by widows and widowers, it is important to recognize that *both* had to make adjustments.

Older widows and widowers have one important life experience in common, the death of a spouse with whom they have had an emotional relationship. Their marriage has been ended. The emotional vacuum created by the death is real to both male and female survivors. They are now single, formerly married people. If they are female, there are numerous widows about their same age. If male, they can identify few widowers. In fact, the mere presence or absence of role models may be one of the most important differences between male and female survivors.

The widows need to make adjustments in day-to-day routines, and they have other widows from whom to seek advice. Bowling and Cartwright (1982) noted that the widows had to cope with grocery shopping for one rather than two. Other widows can give suggestions to the neophyte widow. Feelings of loss can be expressed to another widow who has dealt with a similar life event. Many of the support groups established for widows (e.g., Widows to Widows) are based on the premise that experienced survivors can assist recent survivors with the adjustment to widowhood. For many widows, having another widow with whom to share problems and frustrations is *the* support that helps them move from the crisis to transitional phase.

Widowers, however, have few role models. Generally, they are not associated with many other male survivors. They may know another man who had been widowed but he is probably remarried. Solutions to day-to-day problems are not readily available from former husbands who experienced this life event. Their adjustment is not buttressed with the knowledge that there are other men about the same age who have had to deal with this problem. The larger number of widows also provides a large group of eligible marital partners if a widower wishes to remarry. The widow does not have this luxury. Therefore, as noted in Chapter 1, it is not surprising that many of the widowers remarry.

Concern about the differences between widows and widowers may be better focused on the reorganization of the male *and* female survivors' lives. For the most part, the gender differences in widowhood are related to the definitions of masculinity and femininity. But, differences in adjustments to widowhood transcend gender definitions. Some women and men have developed coping skills to deal with crises. Other men and women have not developed these skills. There is a need to identify characteristics associated with successful adjustment to widowhood for both men and women.

SUMMARY

Widowhood is a family event and the loss reverberates throughout the later life family network. The spouse has lost a mate. Children have lost a parent. Grandchildren no longer have a grandparent. A sibling has lost a brother or sister. The family's interaction patterns and coping skills are related to the ways in which families adjust to a family member's death. The surviving spouse is immediately affected because his/her lifestyle will be radically altered. For some, it is another alteration of their lives because they previously reorganized themselves around the illness of their former spouse. For others, the change is sudden and unexpected.

Immediately following the death of a spouse, the survivor is thrust into a crisis and tends to become isolated. At the same time, children, other relatives and friends rally around the widowed person and assist in many of the day-to-day routines of life. After about six months, the widowed begins to organize life as a single person. The transition entails the development of a new identity and the person begins to cope with everyday decisions and issues. Eventually, after one to two years, the survivor has created a lifestyle as well as is possible without the former spouse. For most older women, the reorganized life does not include a new spouse. For many older men, remarriage is the way in which a new lifestyle is created.

Although there are some differences between the types of adjustments made by widows and widowers, both face a traumatic situation in widowhood. For older people, the death of a spouse marks the end of a long-term marriage. The family's interactions and experiences create rich memories that include the deceased spouse, and the survivor is unable to easily erase them. In widowhood, the temporal marriage is over but it continues in the minds of many male and female survivors.

REVIEW QUESTIONS

(1) What are the different paths to widowhood, and what is the significance of these differences?

(2) What are the major adjustments during the first few months of widowhood?

(3) How do males and females differ in their adjustments to widowhood?

SUGGESTED PROJECTS

(1) Interview your parents and/or grandparents and discuss their perceptions of widowhood. What do they think would be the major adjustments they would expect to make? How can one prepare for widowhood?

(2) If possible, interview someone who has been widowed for a number of years. Discuss the adjustments he or she had to make as a result of widowhood.

CHAPTER
6

The Divorced
and Never Marrieds

Mary, aged 68, has been divorced for 24 years. She has two children, a divorced daughter in her mid-thirties, and a married son, age 30. Her daughter lives four blocks away in an apartment with her two teenaged sons. The son lives in a town two hours away with his wife, two daughters, and one son. Mary is in good health and retired from teaching school three years ago. She had been a school teacher for 28 years. Her steady employment provided the necessary income to raise her two children after her divorce, and she now lives on her teacher's pension and social security income. Her children are very important to her and she sees her daughter and grandsons nearly every day. She also has one meal a week with her son and his family. Since her children are very important to her, she hopes to maintain frequent visits with them. She has an active social life with several widowed and divorced women who are about her age whom she has known for many years. She frequently worries about her health and hopes that her children will be able to care for her if she needs help. However, she does not want to become dependent on her children. Generally she is satisfied with her life and she feels she has coped well as a single person for many years.

Ruth is a 72-year-old woman who has never married. When she was in her early twenties she decided that she did not want to get married because her career was more important to her. She spent several years in graduate school and became a university professor. After thirty years of teaching she retired and became involved in a senior center in her community. Her health has been a problem recently and she believes that she will need to find someone to live with her in the near future. She has a close female friend with whom she has taken vacations for the past 25 years and she has discussed the possibility of their living together. For the past two years they have been helping each other whenever there was a need, and they enjoy each other's company. However, both are concerned about the difficulties of having a roommate after so many years of living alone. Ruth also has a niece and nephew who are very close to her. The niece calls her daily and visits at least once a week. Her nephew's son mows the lawn and paints her house whenever it is needed. She is satisfied with her life and fondly remembers her years as a university professor.

Based on data from the Bureau of Census, approximately one in ten older persons is divorced or has never married. As illustrated in Mary's case, many divorced elderly have children and grandchildren with whom they have frequent contact. Like Ruth, never-married persons frequently interact with siblings, nieces, nephews, and other individuals who are significant to them. This chapter reviews the life situations of the divorced and never married in later life.

First, older divorced persons will be discussed. This is one of the most neglected topics for family and gerontological researchers (Hagestad and Smyer, 1982; Troll et al., 1979). Types of older divorced persons, marital separation of older persons and characteristics of divorced elderly are discussed. The second part of this chapter focuses on older persons who never married. Potential family relationships of older never-married persons are outlined and then the life situations of the never married are explored.

THE DIVORCED IN LATER LIFE

As noted in Chapter 1, the number of divorced elderly has increased somewhat over the past decade. According to census data collected in 1980, about 15 percent of persons aged 65 to 74 years have concluded their first marriage with a divorce (many have remarried, however; this accounts for the difference between this figure and the one mentioned in this chapter's opening paragraph; Glick, 1984). Although the age at which these persons divorced is unknown, it is likely that a large number divorced many years before they entered later life. For example, if a female divorced in her early to mid-thirties, the opportunities for remarriage are less than if she divorced in her twenties. Thus, many persons may be divorced 20 to 25 years before they reach age 55 or 60 years. Approximately 1 percent of all divorces include one person aged 65 years or over (Uhlenberg and Myers, 1981). Projections for the next ten years indicate that the number of older persons who have experienced divorce will increase (Hennon, 1983). For example, it is predicted that approximately one-half of the men and women will terminate their first marriage by divorce before they celebrate their seventy-fifth birthdays (Glick, 1984). If a person divorces when he/she is old, the likelihood of remarriage is low. This is especially true for women.

Types of Divorced in Later Life

The divorced elderly can be categorized into three groups based on the age at which, and the number of times, they have divorced. One group, which we call "career divorced," involves elderly divorced in their early or middle years and never remarried. Like Mary, these individuals have been divorced for many years and enter later life with a long history of being a single person. Many of the divorced women in this category have been responsible for children from their marriages. Since they have raised their children, many enter later life with the support of younger generations as is characteristic of many married elderly. The primary exception is that the family network is abbreviated because there is no husband.

A second category of elderly divorced is the "newly divorced." The men and women have been married for many years, and after the children leave home they obtain a divorce. They may have postponed divorce for many years, and the adjustments associated with a contracting family encouraged them to seek an end to their marriage. For example, a couple may have been dissatisfied with their marriage, but they did not want to divorce as long as they had children at home. When the children left home, their unpleasant marriage was highlighted and they divorced after 25 years of marriage. These individuals enter later life as unmarried persons after many years of being married. Unlike the career divorced, they have not had many years of dealing with singlehood. Most likely, they have children and grandchildren, but now the family organization is altered. They see their children from the perspective of a single person, and they approach their later years without their spouse. Although the proportion who divorce when they are older is small, the lifestyle change for the newly divorced may be intensified by the changes related to getting older. For example, in their middle years, the divorced could rely on their spouses for assistance when they were ill. As older persons, they will need to develop new sources of assistance when they are ill. Unlike many of the never marrieds they may not have lifelong friends on whom they previously depended to provide this type of support.

The third group of divorced elderly is the "serial divorced." These older men and women have married and divorced several times during their lifetimes. They either enter later life as divorced persons or become divorced again. Most have complex family relationships because they have been married more than once; for example, there may be children from more than one marriage. Unlike the newly divorced, these older persons have experience in being unmarried.

Consequently, they are able to address the stresses of being divorced in later life with some knowledge of what it is like to be unmarried.

Predictions of future divorce rates indicate that the career and serial divorced categories may increase. For example, it is estimated that 61 percent of divorced men and 54 percent of divorced women in their thirties in 1980 will redivorce (Glick, 1984). Career divorce may be a more frequent pattern for women than men. Similar to widows, divorced women are less likely to remarry than men. They may not have the opportunity to remarry because there are many eligible older women and few unmarried older men. Further, men may marry younger women, so the older divorced female is at a particular disadvantage.

The divorced elderly make up a small portion of older people (less than 1 in 10). Although many have family relationships which have been altered as a result of divorce, children and grandchildren are there to provide some support in later life.

There are several types of divorced elderly and the differences between these types are open to speculation. There has been little or no research on the types of divorced persons in later life. It may be that the newly divorced elderly have the most difficult time dealing with later life because they have not had to cope with singlehood for many years. Similar to the suddenly widowed, the newly divorced face their later years alone when they had not planned to do so. The career divorced have had a long time to deal with the feelings associated with termination of marriage and have had opportunities to develop coping strategies. The serial divorced, like the career divorced, have been unmarried before and may be cognizant of the problems they will encounter. All three types of divorced elderly will probably be better off if they have children or grandchildren with whom they have had a vital relationships throughout their lives.

Separation of the Elderly

The separation of older, married couples is a time of crisis. For the newly divorced, marriage has been a way of life for many years and the separation that precedes divorce signifies a time of radical change. Even if the marriage was marked with conflict and unhappiness, separation is a transition period during which the couple is faced with changes in lifestyle as well as their individual identities.

It may have been a marriage lasting 25 years with two grown children; now the wife is alone. The husband may have relied on the wife to carry out domestic tasks, and now he must care for himself. It is likely that the longer the marriage and the older the couple, the more difficult the adjustment during the separation period.

Chiriboga (1982) examined the adjustments of younger and older married persons during the separation period. For both younger and older persons, the separation period is characterized by major changes— persons aged 50 years and older had lower morale scores than younger persons. In fact, one in five of the older women and one in six of the older men stated that they were "not too happy." The older persons were more depressed than the younger; also, the older, separated persons were more dissatisfied and less optimistic about the future.

One of the primary activities of separated persons is participation in social activities as an unmarried person. When they were married, going out to eat or attending parties were events which usually included both the husband and wife. With separation, the same activities need to be accomplished as an unmarried person. Older separated persons have more difficulty being a single person in these types of activities than do younger, separated persons.

Generally, the older separated persons were

> more unhappy and reported fewer positive emotional experiences. Their dealings with the social world appeared more tortured, there were more signs of personal discomfort, and their perceptions of the past and future reflected both greater pessimism and long-term dissatisfaction [Chiriboga, 1982: 113].

Separation is a traumatic experience for any married couple because it is a period of change. For older persons, many of whom have a long marital history, separation is stressful. The many years of marriage and establishment of routines and identities as married persons contribute to the increased vulnerability of older persons during separation. Thus, both older men and women find separation a difficult period.

Characteristics of Divorced Elderly

The dissolution of a long-term relationship is a complex event. A couple that has been married for a number of years does not simply decide to discontinue their relationship and seek a legal decree of divorce; rather, the couple's relationship has a history culminating in the termination of their marriage. They may have an emotional commitment to one another that is not eradicated by a legal document. Further, it is likely that they did not arrive at the divorce decision simultaneously. Probably, one spouse wanted the divorce while the other tried to comprehend what was happening to the marriage. For people of any age, divorce is a difficult event.

Since couples are bonded together in various ways, the timing of the divorce is important (Hagestad and Smyer, 1982). There is an emotional bond between the husband and wife as well as a role identity. The role identity refers to the marital partners' identification as "husband" or "wife." In addition, there are the bonds established by the daily routines that married couples develop. According to Hagestad and Smyer (1982) an "orderly divorce" consists of the severing of the emotional bond, then redefinition as an "ex-husband" or "ex-wife," and, finally, the re-establishment of daily routines excluding the spouse. The termination of long-term relationships are particularly difficult because the individuals may experiences mid-life reordering of their lives. Also, compared with younger persons, there are few older divorced persons to assist them in their transition from the married to the unmarried situations.

Hagestad and Symer's study of 43 divorced men and 50 divorced women aged 41 to 61 years indicated that the majority had orderly divorces. Women are more likely to recognize problems within their marriages and discuss their problems with other people than are men. Consequently, women initiated the transition period earlier than men. Those who experienced a disorderly divorce varied considerably. Three couples had a legal divorce but continued to live together; some were emotionally attached to their former mates but they were no longer living together nor sharing daily routines. Still others wanted to share routines but were not emotionally involved. This study clearly illustrates that the termination of a long-term marriage by divorce is complex and multifaceted. Further, one of the most important factors related to adjustment after divorce is the opportunity for a transition period. After a long marriage, persons need time to reorganize their lives.

Even though many divorced persons adjust to unmarried life after a period of time, divorced older persons are not as satisfied with many areas of their lives when compared to married or widowed elderly (Uhlenberg and Myers, 1981). Divorced persons, especially women, of all ages generally experience a worsening of their financial situations and divorced older persons are no exceptions. Consequently, it is not surprising that separated and divorced older persons are the least satisfied with their financial situations when compared to married or widowed older people. The divorced elderly are less satisfied with their social relationships (friends, relatives) than are their married or widowed counterparts.

One study (Hennon, 1983) compared divorced and widowed elderly to identify similarities and differences. Few differences were found in the health situations, fears of declining health and dependency, feelings of powerlessness and alienation, and satisfaction with life. However, compared to the widowed, the divorced elderly had lower incomes, more money worries, were less satisfied with their financial situation, less religious, and were less integrated in their kinship network.

The impact of divorce on an older person's social network is open to speculation. In the case of the newly divorced, children and friends may be divided in their loyalties to the divorced husband and wife. For example, some of the children may provide support to their mother while others side with their father. A child's neutrality may be difficult to achieve in the newly divorced situation. However, the career divorced may have developed a viable support network because they have been divorced for many years. The children, raised by the single parent, will probably provide assistance. The serial divorced may have many potential persons within their support network but their willingness to help may vary. It is likely that the children, if any, and friends of the most recent relationship will help the older, serial divorced persons.

Generally, divorced elderly are not as well off as their married or widowed counterparts. They have more financial difficulties and their adjustment to the single life may be problematic. Although no studies have compared the different types (newly, career, or serial) of divorced, it is likely that there are unique patterns associated with each type. Also, there have been no investigations focusing on the differences between older male and female divorced. Without a doubt, the elderly divorced are neglected by researchers.

OLDER NEVER-MARRIED PERSONS

In our society, most individuals marry at least once within their lifetimes. The persons who never marry characterize less than 8 percent of the older population and will probably continue to represent a minority of older persons. Ruth, in the case at the beginning of this chapter, illustrates an older unmarried female. She was committed to her career and developed close relationships with her niece and nephew as well as with a friend. As with Ruth, family and confidant relationships are important to never-married older persons.

Family Life of Older Never Marrieds

Without a spouse and offspring, the family life of never marrieds revolves around parents, siblings, nieces, nephews, and other persons who are defined as kin. Unlike married older people, never marrieds develop a family life which is not restricted by the boundaries of the nuclear unit. Family events are celebrated with a variety of individuals who are seen as important by the older person. Many times, these persons become members of the single person's support network in later life.

Older never-married persons may have close relationships with their parents that evolved over the years. The unmarried child, especially if female, may become a primary caregiver for older, dependent persons. In fact, in some subcultures such as the Amish or Mennonites, an unmarried daughter is *expected* to care for older parents. In other instances, the older parents may have fewer health problems than the younger unmarried person and provide the necessary assistance. The parental generation is one source of family life for the unmarried older person.

An unmarried person's family life also revolves around siblings and their families. A brother or sister may share family events with the unmarried individual. Inclusion in family activities and celebrations may establish a reciprocal relationship between the unmarried person and his/her nieces or nephews. For example, unmarried women and bachelors may give special gifts or provide lodging on a long-term basis to their siblings' children. Nieces and nephews may mow the lawn or run errands for an older unmarried aunt or uncle. Also, unmarried older persons and their siblings, nieces, and nephews may participate as a family in celebrations such as Christmas, birthdays, or retirements.

A third source of family life for unmarried older men and women involves individuals who are treated as family. In Chapter 4 these individuals were defined as "fictive kin." Throughout their lifetimes, unmarried persons may have developed close relationships with individuals who are not relatives but who they define as family. As close friends, they have shared many things and in later life they may decide to reside together if one becomes dependent. Or they may engage in other activities such as going on trips together. Fictive kin are a source of emotional support for the unmarried in later life.

When considering the never-married older person, it is important to look beyond the nuclear family. The never marrieds create intimate relationships with individuals who are supportive in later life. Even though never marrieds do not have a spouse or children, they have the potential for an active family life in later life. As Ward (1979: 868) noted,

> the family is an important supportive institution in the lives of older people, helping counteract the shrinkage in social networks which may accompany aging. Rather than being less dependent upon this, the never-married may be more so because of the fluidity and tenuousness of their lifestyles.

However, the life situation of the never marrieds may be affected by the absence of a spouse and children.

Life Situations of the Never Married

What is the life situation of older never-married persons? Are they as happy, healthy, and financially well off as their married counterparts? One study of never-married older people suggests that feelings of happiness are decreased in later life (Ward, 1979). In the younger years, the never marrieds lead a more exciting life and are happier than married persons. However, in the later years, the never married are less happy than husbands and wives. Their excitement at life also declines as the unmarried persons enters old age. Generally, the never marrieds experience decreased happiness and excitement so that they are very similar to widowed and divorced older persons, while the marrieds are the happiest and view life with the most excitement.

While there is a decrease in the overall happiness of never-married persons in later life, many do report satisfaction with their lifestyles. For example, Gubrium (1975) reported that older never married persons view their lifestyles as a ordinary extension of their upbringing and life goals. Some may not have wanted to marry, as one stated, "I was brought up very strict. I'm very much against marriage. I could never find somebody I liked. If you get married and still have to work, you might as well stay single" (Gubrium, 1975: 37). Another stated, "I've never been married. I've been perfectly satisfied. I've been independent and found my niche. I earned my living all my life and I never said, 'Give me, give me!' You don't have to marry to be happy. I don't think I would marry. I made a good choice" (Gubrium, 1975: 36). As a group, never-married older persons may be less happy than married older persons, but some never-married women and bachelors are quite satisfied with their lives.

The only difference in the health situation is that married persons view their health slightly more positively than do never-married persons (Ward, 1979). The financial situation is also more complex. Older married persons report higher *family incomes* than do older single men and women. However, the *individual income* of the unmarrieds exceeds that of the marrieds. The highest individual income is reported by single women. Consequently, the higher individual income for the never marrieds is surpassed by the combined incomes of husband and wives. In terms of health and financial situation, there are no significant differences between the never marrieds and married persons.

Not surprisingly, never-married persons are more likely to be living alone. Contrary to the popular belief that never-married persons are more involved in community activities and other voluntary associations, Ward found that the never marrieds were not more likely to participate in these activities. Involvement in work is important to many individuals but it is particularly crucial to never-married persons. Consequently, retirement has a particularly negative effect on them. Ward reported that never-married older persons had more difficulty adjusting to later life without involvement in work. The absence of spouse and children is related to lower involvement with family (Ward, 1979; Longino and Lipman, 1982). However, neither study explored the various alternative sources of family life noted above.

Clearly, never marrieds are a group of our older population that has been neglected by gerontological and family researchers. Apparently, they have developed a lifestyle that is particularly successful in the early and middle years of adulthood. However, in later life they seem to experience disadvantages compared to their married counterparts. Even though they have the potential to develop family relationships, their family network and frequency of family contact is more restricted. The presence of a spouse and children is a convenience that never marrieds do not have. After retirement and as health problems create more dependency on others, the never marrieds appear to experience the most difficulty.

SUMMARY

Mary and Ruth represent two small groups of older persons. Over the next twenty years, we can expect more divorced and never-married older persons. Even though there is limited research on these groups, it is clear that they have developed family relationships beyond the traditional nuclear family unit. Many of the divorced, older persons have children, and they receive emotional support from them. Never-married older persons have the potential to establish family life relationships with their parents, siblings, nieces, nephews, and fictive kin.

These lifestyles are particularly intriguing because, in many instances, they represent independent persons who are becoming vulnerable to the dependencies of aging. Their adaptations and strategies for dealing with these dependencies may provide suggestions for married and widowed older persons. As noted in Chapter 1, many married older persons will probably become single as a result of widowhood. Individuals like Mary and Ruth may provide examples for coping with singlehood in later life.

REVIEW QUESTIONS

(1) What are the different types of divorced older persons?

(2) What are the problems associated with separation of a long-term marriage?

(3) How do you describe the lifestyles of older divorced persons?

(4) Who are potential members of the never marrieds' family network?

(5) How do never-married and married older persons compare?

SUGGESTED PROJECTS

(1) Discuss the differences and similarities between divorced and never-married older persons. What are the advantages and disadvantages of each group? How do they compare to married older persons?

(2) Interview an older divorced person and an older never-married person. Compare their lifestyles. Write a case study of each person, noting his or her satisfactions, problems, joys, and ways of coping with singlehood in later life.

CHAPTER

7

Later Life Families in the Future

LATER LIFE FAMILY RELATIONSHIPS have been described as vital and resilient in the midst of the changes associated with later life. Married couples, children and grandchildren, divorced and single older persons have family relationships that continue into the later years. In this chapter, observations concerning the continuity of later life family relationships are discussed, as are the feelings of affection and obligations between family members, and the increased complexity of later life family relationships. Other topics include technology and later life families, long-term care of older family members, bureaucracy and the older family, and service delivery to later life families.

CONTINUITY OF FAMILY RELATIONSHIPS

Family relationships in later life are an extension of previous family interactions within the family network. The continuous nature of these relationships permeates all family relationships in later life. For instance, older persons who are spouses have a long history of interacting with each other. Or, older parents establish patterns of communication and affection with their children long before they can be considered later life families. Older siblings develop traditions that are shared many years before they enter the later years. Also, older never-married and divorced persons have long-term friendships and kinship relationships. Consequently, most family relationships are premised on a long history of contact and, in most instances, individuals can be expected to continue these patterns into later life.

The discussion of older couple relationships in Chapter 2 provides several illustrations of the continuity of later life family relationships. Older couples divide responsibility for household tasks much as they did in their middle years. Retirement and the subsequent increased opportunity for sharing responsibility do not seem to alter household patterns significantly. Declining health is the only factor related to a modification of previous divisions of household responsibility.

A second example of the continuity of later life relationships is the sexual activity and interest of older men and women. Older people who were interested and participated in sexual behavior during their middle years are likely to continue these interests and activities into their later years. Again, health is a factor that may alter the participation of older persons in sexual activity.

Marital satisfaction is a third characteristic that evidences a continuous pattern. Satisfied couples in their middle years are likely to be satisfied in their later years. Those who have found marriage to be more rewarding with each life stage will probably report that the later years are also more rewarding. For others whose marriages have not been satisfying, later life will probably bring a decrease in satisfaction.

In each of these examples, the patterns evidenced in the later years were established before the family evolved to the later stages of the family life cycle. Thus older persons are equipped to deal with the life changes in the later years (e.g., children leaving home, retirement). Their coping strategies have been developed over the many years of interacting within the family. Therefore, when they are confronted with life changes, they usually can adapt adjustment mechanisms that they have used in their early or middle years.

The importance of continuity in interaction and coping strategies should not be minimized. Younger family members may be better able to understand an older person's behavior if they remember how the older person previously responded in similar situations. Also, individuals who want to assist a dependent older family member may need to know about the older person's family history. Families develop patterns of interaction and behavior that influence later life family relationships.

Although the continuity of family relationships is underscored, it should not be interpreted that family relationships cannot be altered in later life. Changes in these family relationships are possible and will most likely occur when the family members make a concerted effort to modify previous patterns. In most cases, recognition of the long history of family interaction facilitates changes in family interactions.

AFFECTION AND OBLIGATION IN LATER LIFE FAMILIES

The research reviewed in Chapters 3 and 4 indicates that there is a vital, reciprocal relationship between older parents, adult children, and grandchildren. Generally, regular and frequent interaction and assistance flows both ways between the generations. Some evidence suggests that adult children help their parents when they are ill even if there is not a close affectional relationship between them. In many ways it appears that adult children feel obligated to assist their dependent parents.

Feelings of obligation may be based on the younger generation's desire to pay back their parents for raising them. Therefore, if a mother becomes widowed, adult children may rally around her to provide emotional support even though they have not had a close relationship. However, data do not address the issue of the relationship between obligation and *continual care* of a dependent parent. It is not surprising that during a crisis period such as widowhood or illness adult children provide assistance. However, feelings of obligation may not be sufficient to encourage continual care of an older person.

Affection for the older person may become an important factor in deciding whether to establish a multigenerational family. An adult child who feels obligated may buy groceries or visit an older parent. But an adult child who feels obligation *and* deep affection for the older parent may visit daily and eventually ask the parent to move into his/her home. Consequently, affectional ties may provide the stimulus for adult children to provide 24-hour care rather than move a dependent parent into a nursing home.

Since intergenerational relationships are usually reciprocal, it is likely that obligation and affection regulate the flow of assistance from parents to children. While parents may visit, give gifts, and help adult children in other ways because they are their children, they may do more when they especially like their child and his/her family. The reciprocal relationships between the generations are bonded by obligation and fueled by affection.

INCREASED COMPLEXITY OF
OLDER FAMILY RELATIONSHIPS

Family relationships of older people are expected to become more complex in the future. With the current divorce rate and increased lifespan of men and women, family relationships will become more complicated. For example, as noted in Chapter 3, divorce creates complicated linkages in a family network. For example, the generational relationships may be affected by the development of step-grandparents or step-grandchildren. For older people, these changes in the family network may pull them closer or push them away from their adult children and their families. The patterns of interaction and support between the generations in these families may be different from families in which divorce has not occurred.

As the older generation increases in age, there is an increased likelihood of more generations within the family. Consequently, there are more members of the family with whom to interact. Family celebrations bring these generations together. The impact of these multiple younger generations on the well-being of the older generations is open to speculation, but the older generation very likely feels proud of the younger generations. At the same time, they may not have the energy to enter into close relationships with their great-grandchildren. The flow of support from these younger generations is not precisely defined. The great-grandchildren may perform chores for their older relatives, or they may view them as distant relatives. In any case, the increased complexity of the family is clearly demonstrated when there is a family celebration which every generation attends. In terms of energy, time, and space, the 90-year old woman may not be able to accommodate her family any more. The next younger generation may need to do the organizing. This change may be difficult for the 90-year old woman. The complexity of the family network may be overwhelming or it may be a joy to see the expanded size of the family. It is likely that the closeness of the generations will relate to the ways in which older persons deal with the increased complexity of later life families.

TECHNOLOGY AND LATER LIFE FAMILIES

Technological advances in communication may modify the long-term care of older persons. For example, it may soon be possible to provide some medical care at home and communicate information from the home to the doctor via a computer line. This will permit a person to be treated for health problems at home that would have previously required hospitalization. This increased home care will affect family relationships in later life. On the one hand, spouses may be able to care for each other at home longer and not be separated by institutional constraints. On the other hand, the primary caregivers will not be relieved of their caregiving responsibilities as they were when the dependent person entered the hospital. Social services may need to be developed to deal with the problems of the long-term family caregivers.

Development of technological advances that prolong longevity needs to include a consideration of the implications for social relationships. For some families, the technology will allow them to continue vital relationships. For others, the caregiving tasks will exacerbate the tenuous bonds on which their relationships are based. In either case, family relationships in later life are affected by the development of new technology for dealing with health problems.

LONG-TERM CARE OF OLDER FAMILY MEMBERS

Since older people aged 75 years and above are growing in numbers, long-term care of older family members will be an increasingly important concern. Families will need to be equipped to deal with the physical, financial, and emotional costs associated with caring for someone who has health problems. As noted in Chapter 3, the relationships between older family members and health care institutions are complex. Institutional policies may encourage or discourage family involvement. Home care can create extraordinary burdens on many families.

As Brubaker and Brubaker (1984) outlined, concern can be focused on the matching of long-term care services with the needs of the older person as well as other family members. The needs of the entire family need to be assessed so that the care plan involves the family. Generally, long-term care of an older person involves the long-term care of the family. This type of family perspective may help relieve some of the stresses and frustrations families feel as they deal with the health problems of their older members.

BUREAUCRACY AND LATER LIFE
FAMILY RELATIONSHIPS

The relationship between bureaucracies and later life families has been identified by several writers (Sussman, 1977; Streib and Beck,

1980). As the family seeks care for a dependent member outside the family unit, contact with bureaucratic organizations is inevitable. Nursing homes, hospitals, home care, and social security benefits are managed by a bureaucracy; private and public organizations are designed around the standardization of a bureaucracy. Presently, later life families cannot avoid contact with these organizations, and in the future, contact is likely to increase.

Families and bureaucracies are strange bedfellows even though they cannot live without each other (Sussman, 1977). Families are primary groups oriented toward individual activity and concerns; they consist of long-term relationships and respond to problems requiring little specialized knowledge. Bureaucracies are secondary groups that are not concerned about the length of the relationship nor about the peculiarities of the individual. Problems requiring specialized knowledge and expertise are dealt with by bureaucracies.

When families and bureaucracies meet, their goals and communications may not agree. For example, when a family member enters a hospital, the family is required to complete many forms requesting information that may or may not be related to the admission. The doctor may discuss the problem with the family members but they may not understand the technical information nor the ramifications of the problem. They may complain that their family member is not given enough individual attention. Many times the confusion is a consequence of the different orientations of families and bureaucracies.

For older family members, bureaucracies are mediated by others, usually spouses, siblings, or adult children. In the above example, an adult child with some medical training may translate the doctor's comments so that the family will understand their older member's situation. In another situation, an adult child may identify various nursing homes as an alternative living situation for older parents. The adult child may become a negotiator with the nursing home choosen by the parents. The adult child may have more experience with bureaucracies than the parents. In any case, adult children become the mediators between the older family member and bureaucracy.

Future interactions between families and bureaucracies are likely to continue in a similar fashion. However, the older dependent person may have more knowledge about bureaucracies and rely less on younger generations as mediators. Bureaucratic organizations will continue, and their influence on the everyday lives of older family members will probably increase as knowledge becomes more specialized. In the future families will become astute about ways to advocate for their older members.

SERVICE DELIVERY TO LATER LIFE FAMILIES

In the future more service and service providers will be working with older persons and their families. Nurses, doctors, social workers, health care personnel, and others will be needed to provide assistance to the growing number of older persons. Information about older people and their families has expanded greatly since many of these service providers received their training, and their knowledge of older people may be limited (Barresi and Brubaker, 1979; Brubaker and Barresi, 1979). The more experience they have with older people, the more knowledgeable they become about providing their services to older family members. Thus, the increase in service use by older persons will be accompanied by an increase in knowledge about how to tailor services to the older population.

When providing services to older persons, it is important to view them as members of family networks (E. Brubaker, 1983). The older person is not alone and family members are concerned. Services can be provided to both the older person *and* his/her family. As noted in Chapter 6, the family may refer to persons other than spouse or children. Service providers need to have a broad definition of family and seek to enhance the family's support of their older members.

SUMMARY

Family relationships in later life are alive and well for many persons. The older generation has established vital relationships with children, grandchildren, and others who provide extraordinary support in later life. Older divorced and never marrieds have family networks that also provide support. Later life family relationships will frequently face interactions with bureaucracies in the future. The family as mediator will probably continue and its importance may be increased.

Later life family relationships are particularly interesting because they represent long-term relationships. For example, sibling relationships exist for a lifetime; spouse relationships may continue for more than half a century; parent-child relationships may exist for nearly 50 years. In a society marked with change, it is remarkable that the later life family is characterized by mutual interaction, respect, and support. Even when divorce or death terminates some family relationships, there is frequent contact in later life families. Later life families are a positive commentary on the strength of the family in our society.

REVIEW QUESTIONS

(1) What evidence supports the continuity of later life family relationships?

(2) How do feelings of affection and obligation affect later life family relationships?

(3) How will later life family relationships become more complex?

(4) What effect does technology have on family relationships in later life?

(5) What are the differences between families and bureaucracies? How do these differences affect later life families?

SUGGESTED PROJECTS

(1) Examine your own family and identify patterns that you think will continue as you get older. How will these patterns affect your relationships in later life?

(2) Interview some persons who provide services to older people about their views of later life family relationships. Develop suggestions on how to strengthen family relationships while providing services to older persons.

References

ADAMS, B. N. (1968) Kinship in an Urban Setting. Chicago: Markham.
ADE-RIDDER, L. and T. H. BRUBAKER (1983) "The quality of long-term marriages," in T. H. Brubaker (ed.) Family Relationships in Later Life. Beverly Hills, CA: Sage.
ALLAN, G. (1977) "Sibling solidarity." Journal of Marriage and the Family 39: 177-184.
ANDERSON, S. A., C. S. RUSSELL, and W. A. SCHUMM (1983) "Perceived marital quality and family life-cycle categories: a further analysis." Journal of Marriage and the Family 45: 127-139.
ANDERSON, T. B. (1984) "Widowhood as a life transition: its impact on kinship ties." Journal of Marriage and the Family 46: 105-114.
ARD, B. N. (1977) "Sex in lasting marriages: a longitudinal study." Journal of Sex Research 13: 274-285.
ARENS, D. A. (1982-1983) "Widowhood and well-being: an examination of sex differences within a causal model." International Journal of Aging and Human Development 15: 27-40.
ATCHLEY, R. C. (1980) Social Forces in Later Life. Belmont, CA: Wadsworth.
——— (1976) Sociology of Retirement. Cambridge, MA: Schenkman.
——— and S. J. MILLER (1983) "Types of elderly couples," in T. H. Brubaker (ed.) Family Relationships in Later Life. Beverly Hills, CA: Sage.
AXELSON, L. J. (1960) "Personal adjustment in the postparental period." Marriage and Family Living 22: 66-68.
BACHRACH, C. A. (1980) "Childlessness and social isolation among the elderly." Journal of Marriage and the Family 42: 627-637.
BALLWEG, J. A. (1967) "Resolution of conjugal role adjustment after retirement." Marriage and Family Living 29: 277-281.
BANKOFF, E. A. (1983) "Social support and adaptation to widowhood." Journal of Marriage and the Family 45: 827-839.
BARRESI, C. M. and T. H. BRUBAKER (1979) "Clinical social workers' knowledge about aging: responses to the 'Facts on Aging' quiz." Journal of Gerontological Social Work 2: 137-146.
BECKMAN, L. J. and B. B. HOUSER (1982) "The consequences of childlessness on the social-psychological well-being of older women." Journal of Gerontology 37: 243-250.
BERARDO, F. M. (1970) "Survivorship and social isolation: the case of the aged widower." Family Coordinator 19: 11-25.
BLENKNER, M. (1965) "Social work and family relationships in later life with some thoughts on filial maturity," in E. Shanas and G. F. Streib (eds.) Social Structure and the Family. Englewood Cliffs, NJ: Prentice-Hall.
BLOOD, R. O., Jr., and D. M. WOLFE (1960) Husbands and Wives. New York: Macmillan.
BOWLING, A. and A. CARTWRIGHT (1982) Life After a Death. New York: Tavistock.
BRAITO, R. and D. ANDERSON (1981) "Singles and aging: implications for needed research," in P. J. Stein (ed.) Single Life: Unmarried Adults in Social Context. New York: St. Martin's.
BRIM, O. G., Jr. (1976) "Theories of the male midlife crisis." Counseling Psychologist 6: 2-9.
BRODY, E. (1981) "Women in the middle and family help to older people." Gerontologist 21: 471-480.
BROTMAN, H. B. (1981) Supplement to the Chartbook on Aging in America. Washington, DC: White House Conference on Aging.
BRUBAKER, E. (1983) "Providing services to older persons and their families," in T. H. Brubaker (ed.) Family Relationships in Later Life. Beverly Hills, CA: Sage.

BRUBAKER, T. H. (1985) "Responsibility for household tasks: a look at golden anniversary couples aged 75 years and older," in W. Peterson and J. Quadagno (eds.) Social Bonds in Later Life. Beverly Hills, CA: Sage.

———[ed.] (1983) Family Relationships in Later Life. Beverly Hills, CA: Sage.

———and C. M. BARRESI (1979) "Social workers' levels of knowledge about old age and perceptions of service delivery to the elderly." Research on Aging 1: 213-231.

BRUBAKER, T. H. and E. BRUBAKER (1984) "Family support of older persons in the long term care setting: recommendations for practice," in W. H. Quinn and G. A. Hughston (eds.) Independent Aging: Perspectives in Social Gerontology. Rockville, MD: Aspen Systems.

———(1981) "Adult child and elderly parent household: issues in stress for theory and practice." Alternative Lifestyles 4: 242-256.

BRUBAKER, T. H. and C. B. HENNON (1982) "Responsibility for household tasks: comparing dual earner and dual retired marriages," in M. Szinovacz (ed.) Women's Retirement: Policy Implications of Recent Research. Beverly Hills, CA: Sage.

CAMERON, P. (1976) "Masculinity/femininity of the generations: as self-reported as stereotypically appraised." International Journal of Aging and Human Development 7: 143-151.

———(1969) "The 'life-force' and age." Journal of Gerontology 24: 199-200.

———(1968) "Masculinity/femininity of the aged." Journal of Gerontology 23: 63-65.

———and H. BIBER (1973) "Sexual thought throughout the lifespan." Gerontologist 13: 144-147.

CHEAL, D. J. (1983) "Intergenerational family transfers." Journal of Marriage and the Family 45: 805-814.

CHIRIBOGA, D. A. (1982) "Adaptation to marital separation in later and earlier life." Journal of Gerontology 37: 109-114.

CICIRELLI, V. G. (1983a) "Adult children's attachment and helping behavior to elderly parents: a path model." Journal of Marriage and the Family 45: 815-824.

———(1983b) "Adult children and their elderly parents," in T. H. Brubaker (ed.) Family Relationships in Later Life. Beverly Hills, CA: Sage.

———(1983c) "A comparison of helping behavior to elderly parents of adult children with intact and disrupted marriages." Gerontologist 23: 619-625.

———(1982) "Sibling influence throughout the lifespan," in M. E. Lamb and B. Sutton-Smith (eds.) Sibling Relationships: Their Nature and Significance Across the Lifespan. Hillsdale, NJ: Lawrence Erlbaum.

———(1981a) Helping Elderly Parents: Role of Adult Children. Boston: Auburn House.

———(1981b) "Kin relationships of childless and one-child elderly in relation to social services." Journal of Gerontological Social Work 4: 19-33.

———(1980) "Sibling relationships in adulthood: a life span perspective," in L. W. Poon (ed.) Aging in the 1980s: Psychological Issues. Washington, DC: American Psychological Association.

———(1977) "Relationship of siblings to the elderly person's feelings and concerns." Journal of Gerontology 32: 317-322.

CLARK, A. L. and P. WALLIN (1965) "Women's sexual responsiveness and the duration and quality of their marriage." American Journal of Sociology 71: 187-196.

CLARK, M. and B. G. ANDERSON (1967) Culture and Aging. Springfield, IL: Charles Thomas.

CLAVAN, S. (1978) "The impact of social class and social trends on the role of grandparent." Family Coordinator 27: 351-358.

CLEVELAND, W. P. and D. T. GIANTURCO (1976) "Remarriage probability after widowhood: a retrospective method." Journal of Gerontology 31: 99-103.

CORBY, N. and J. ZARIT (1983) "Old and alone: the unmarried in later life," in R. B. Weg (ed.) Sexuality in Later Life. New York: Academic.

CROSSMAN, L., C. LONDON, and C. BARRY (1981) "Older women caring for disabled spouses: a model for supportive services." Gerontologist 21: 464-470.

DeNICOLA, P. and M. PERUZZA (1974) "Sex in the aged." Journal of the American Geriatric Society 22: 380-382.

DENTLER, R. A. and P. PINEO (1960) "Sexual adjustment, marital adjustment, and personal growth of husbands: a panel analysis." Marriage and Family Living 22: 45-48.

DEUTSCHER, I. (1964) "The quality of post-parental life." Journal of Marriage and the Family 26: 52-60.

DOBSON, C. (1983) "Sex-role and marital role expectations," in T. H. Brubaker (ed.) Family Relationships in Later Life. Beverly Hills, CA: Sage.

DOWD, J. J. and V. L. BENGTSON (1978) "Aging in minority populations: an examination of the double jeopardy hypothesis." Journal of Gerontology 33: 427-436.

DRESSEL, P. L. (1980) "Assortive mating in later life: some initial considerations." Alternative Lifestyles 1: 379-396.

DUVALL, E. M. (1977) Marriage and Family Development. Philadelphia: J. B. Lippincott.

FENGLER, A. P. (1975) "Attitudinal orientation of wives toward their husbands' retirement." International Journal of Aging and Human Development 6: 139-152.

———and N. GOODRICH (1979) "Wives of elderly disabled men: the hidden patients." Gerontologist 19: 175-183.

FISHER, L. R. (1983) "Transition into grandmotherhood." International Journal of Aging and Human Development 16: 67-78.

FOSTER, D., L. KLINGER-VARTABEDIAN, and L. WISPE (1984) "Male longevity and age differences between spouses." Journal of Gerontology 39: 117-120.

FOX, J., L. BULUSU, and L. KINDEN (1979) "Mortality and age differences in marriage." Journal of Biosocial Science 11: 117-131.

GARZA, J. M. and P. L. DRESSEL (1983) "Sexuality and later life marriages," in T. H. Brubaker (ed.) Family Relationships in Later Life. Beverly Hills, CA: Sage.

GLENN, N. D. (1975) "Psychological well-being in the post-parental stage: some evidence from national surveys." Journal of Marriage and the Family 37: 105-110.

GLICK, P. C. (1984) "Marriage, divorce, and living arrangements: prospective changes." Journal of Family Issues 5: 7-26.

———(1979) "The future marital status and living arrangements of the elderly." Gerontologist 19: 301-309.

———(1977) "Updating the life cycle of the family." Journal of Marriage and the Family 39: 5-14.

———and A. J. NORTON (1977) "Marrying, divorcing, and living together in the U.S. Today." Population Bulletin 32: 1-39.

GREENE, V. L. and D. J. MONAHAN (1982) "The impact of visitation on patient well-being in nursing homes." Gerontologist 22: 418-423.

GUBRIUM, J. F. (1975) "Being single in old age." International Journal of Aging and Human Development 6: 29-41.

———(1974) "Marital desolation and the evaluation of everyday life in old age." Journal of Marriage and the Family 36: 107-113.

GUTMANN, D. L. (1977) "The cross-cultural perspective: notes towards a comparative psychology of aging," in J. E. Birren and K. W. Schaie (eds.) Handbook of the Psychology of Aging. New York: Van Nostrand Reinhold.

———(1975) "Parenthood: key to comparative psychology of the life cycle," in N. Datan and L. Ginsberg (eds.) Developmental Psychology: Normative Life Crisis. New York: Academic.

HACKER, A. (1983) US: A Statistical Portrait of the American People. New York: Viking Press, Penguin Books.

HAGESTAD, G. O. (1981) "Problems and promises in the social psychology of intergenerational relations," in R. W. Fogel et al. (eds.) Aging: Stability and Change in the Family. New York: Academic.

———and M. SMYER (1982) "Dissolving long-term relationships: patterns of divorcing in middle age," in S. Duck (ed.) Personal Relationships 4: Dissolving Personal Relationships. New York: Academic.

HANSON, S. L., W. J. SAUER, and W. C. SEELBACH (1983) "Racial and cohort variations in filial responsibility norms." Gerontologist 23: 626-631.

Louis Harris and Associates (1975) Myths and Realities of Aging in America. Washington, DC: National Council on Aging.

HARTSHORNE, T. S. and G. J. MANASTER (1982) "The relationship with grandparents: contact, importance, role conceptions." International Journal of Aging and Human Development 15: 233-245.

HAYS, J. A. (1984) "Aging and family resources: availability and proximity of kin." Gerontologist 24: 149-153.

HEINEMANN, G. D. (1983) "Family involvement and support for widowed persons," in T. H. Brubaker (ed.) Family Relationships in Later Life. Beverly Hills, CA: Sage.

HENNON, C. B. (1983) "Divorce and the elderly: a neglected area of research," in T. H. Brubaker (ed.) Family Relationships in Later Life. Beverly Hills, CA: Sage.

———T. H. BRUBAKER, and S. A. BAUMANN (1983) "Your aging parent: deciding whether to live together." Cooperative Extension Service Bulletin B3245. University of Wisconsin Extension, Madison.

HENRETTE, J. C. and A. M. O'RAND (1980) "Labor force participation of older married women." Social Security Bulletin 43: 10-16.

HERR, J. J. and J. H. WEAKLAND (1979) Counseling Elders and Their Families. New York: Springer.

HESS, B. and J. M. WARING (1978) "Changing patterns of aging and family bonds in later life." Family Coordinator 27: 303-314.

HEYMAN, D. K. and F. C. JEFFERS (1968) "Wives and retirement: a pilot study." Journal of Gerontology 23: 488-496.

HICKS, M. W. and M. PLATT (1970) "Marital happiness and stability: a review of the sixties." Journal of Marriage and the Family 32: 553-573.

HILL, R. B. (1978) "A demographic profile of the black elderly." Aging 287-288: 2-9.

HOFFMAN, E. (1979-1980) "Young adults' relations with their grandparents: an exploratory study." International Journal of Aging and Human Development 10: 299-310.

HOLAHAN, C. K. (1984) "Marital attitudes over 40 years: a longitudinal and cohort analysis." Journal of Gerontology 39: 49-57.

HOOK, W. F., J. SOBAL, and J. C. OAK (1982) "Frequency of visitation in nursing homes: patterns of contact across the boundaries of total institutions." Gerontologist 22: 424-428.

HUTCHISON, I. W. (1975) "The significance of marital status for morale and life satisfaction among lower-income elderly." Journal of Marriage and the Family 37: 287-293.

HYMAN, H. H. (1983) Of Time and Widowhood. Durham, NC: Duke University Press.

JACKSON, J. J. (1972a) "Comparative life styles and family-friend relationships among older black women." Family Coordinator 21: 477-485.

———(1972b) "Marital life among aging blacks." Family Coordinator 21: 21-27.

JOHNSON, C. L. and D. J. CATALANO (1981) "Childless elderly and their family supports." Gerontologist 21: 610-618.

JOHNSON, E. (1981) "Role expectations and role realities of older Italian mothers and their daughters." International Journal of Aging and Human Development 14: 271-276.

KAHANA, B. and E. KAHANA (1970) "Grandparenthood from the perspective of the developing grandchild." Developmental Psychology 3: 98-105.

KEATING, N. C. and P. COLE (1980) "What do I do with him 24 hours a day? Changes in the housewife role after retirement." Gerontologist 20: 84-89.

KEITH, P. M. and T. H. BRUBAKER (1979) "Male household roles in later life: a look at masculinity and marital relationships." Family Coordinator 28: 497-502.

KINSEY, A. C., W. B. POMEROY, C. R. MARTIN, and P. H. GEBHARD (1953) Sexual Behavior in the Human Female. Philadelphia: Saunders.

KIVETT, V. R. and R. M. LEARNER (1980) "Perspectives on the childless rural elderly: a comparative analysis." Gerontologist 20: 708-716.

KIVNICK, H. Q. (1982) "Grandparenthood: an overview of meaning and mental health." Gerontologist 22: 59-66.

KOHEN, J. A. (1983) "Old but not alone: informal social supports among the elderly by marital status and sex." Gerontologist 23: 57-63.

LEE, G. R. (1978) "Marriage and morale in later life." Journal of Marriage and the Family 40: 131-139.

———and E. ELLITHORPE (1982) "Intergenerational exchange and subjective well-being among the elderly." Journal of Marriage and the Family 44: 217-224.

LIPMAN, A. (1962) "Role conceptions of couples in retirement," in C. Tibbets and W. Donahue (eds.) Social and Psychological Aspects of Aging. New York: Columbia University Press.

———(1961) "Role conceptions and morale of couples in retirement." Journal of Gerontology 16: 267-271.

LIVSON, F. B. (1983) "Gender identity: a life-span view of sex role development," in Ruth B. Weg (ed.) Sexuality in the Later Years. New York: Academic.

LOCKER, R. (1981) "Institutionalized elderly: understanding and helping couples." Journal of Gerontological Social Work 3: 37-48.

LONGINO, C. F., Jr., and A. LIPMAN (1982) "The married, the formerly married and the never married: support system differentials of older women in planned retirement communities." International Journal of Aging and Human Development 15: 285-297.

———(1981) "Married and spouseless men and women in planned retirement communities: support network differentials." Journal of Marriage and the Family 43: 169-177.

LOPATA, H. Z. (1981) "Widowhood and husband sanctification." Journal of Marriage and the Family 43: 439-450.

———(1979) Women as Widows. New York: Elsevier.

———(1973) Widowhood in an American City. Cambridge, MA: Schenkman.

LOWENTHAL, M. F., M. THURNHER, and D. CHIRIBOGA (1975) Four Stages of Life. San Francisco: Jossey-Bass.

MAAS, H. and J. A. KUYPERS (1977) From Thirty to Seventy. San Francisco: Jossey-Bass.

MATTHEWS, S. H. and J. SPREY (1984) "The impact of divorce on grandparenthood: an exploratory study." Gerontologist 24: 41-47.

McCONNEL, C. E. and F. DELJAVAN (1983) "Consumption patterns of the retired household." Journal of Gerontology 38: 480-490.

McKAIN, W. C. (1972) "A new look at older marriages." Family Coordinator 21: 61-69.

———(1969) Retirement Marriage. Monograph 3. Storrs: Agricultural Experiment Station, University of Connecticut.

MEDLEY, M. L. (1977) "Marital adjustment in the post retirement years." Family Coordinator 26: 5-11.

MILLER, B. C. (1976) "A multivariate development model of marital satisfaction." Journal of Marriage and the Family 38: 643-657.

MINDEL, C. H. (1983) "The elderly in minority families," in T. H. Brubaker (ed.) Family Relationships in Later Life. Beverly Hills, CA: Sage.

———(1979) "Multigenerational family households: recent trends and implications for the future." Gerontologist 19: 456-463.

———and R. WRIGHT (1982) "Satisfaction in multigenerational households." Journal of Gerontology 37: 483-489.

MINNIGERODE, F. A. and J. A. LEE (1978) "Young adults' perceptions of social sex roles across the life span." Sex Roles 4: 563-569.

MITCHELL, J. and J. C. REGISTER (1984) "An exploration of family interaction with the elderly by race, socioeconomic status and residence." Gerontologist 24: 48-54.

MONTGOMERY, J. E. (1982) "The economics of supportive services for families with disabled and aging members." Family Relations 31: 19-27.

MONTGOMERY, R.J.B. (1982) "Impact of institutional care policies on family integration." Gerontologist 22: 54-58.

MOONEY, E. C. (1981) Alone. New York: G. P. Putnam.

MORGAN, L. A. (1980) "Work in widowhood: a viable option?" Gerontologist 20: 581-587.

MOSS, M. S. and S. Z. MOSS (1980) "The image of the deceased spouse in remarriage of elderly widow(er)s." Journal of Gerontological Social Work 3: 59-70.

NEUGARTEN, B. L. and K. WEINSTEIN (1964) "The changing American grandparent." Journal of Marriage and the Family 26: 199-204.

NEUGARTEN, B. L., J. W. MOORE, and J. C. LOWE (1965) "Age norms, age constraints, and adult socialization." American Journal of Sociology 70: 710-717.

NEWMAN, G. and C. R. NICHOLS (1970) "Sexual activities and attitudes in older persons," in E. Palmore (ed.) Normal Aging. Durham, NC: Duke University Press.

NEWMAN, S. (1976) Housing Adjustments of Older People: A Report from the Second Phase. Ann Arbor, MI: Institute for Social Research.

NOELKER, L. and Z. HAREL (1978) "Predictors of well-being and survival among institutionalized aged." Gerontologist 18: 562-567.

ORTHNER, D. K. (1975) "Leisure activity patterns and marital satisfaction over the marital career." Journal of Marriage and the Family 37: 91-102.

PALMORE, E. (1981) Social Patterns in Normal Aging: Findings from the Duke Longitudinal Study. Durham, NC: Duke University Press.

PARKES, C. (1972) Bereavement. London: Tavistock.

PARRON, E. M. and L. E. TROLL (1978) "Golden wedding couples: effects of retirement on intimacy in long-standing marriages." Alternative Lifestyles 1: 447-464.

PEASE, R. A. (1974) "Female professional students and sexuality in an aging male." Gerontologist 14: 153-157.

PETERSON, J. A. and B. PAYNE (1975) Love in the Later Years. New York: Association Press.

PFEIFFER, E., A. VERWOERDT, and G. C. DAVIS (1974) "Sexual behavior in middle life," in E. Palmore (ed.) Normal Aging II. Durham, NC: Duke University Press.

PFEIFFER, E., A. VERWOERDT, and H. S. WANG (1970) "Sexual behavior in aged men and women," in E. Palmore (ed.) Normal Aging. Durham, NC: Duke University Press.

PINEO, P. E. (1969) "Development in the later years of marriage." Family Coordinator 18: 135-140.

———(1961) "Disenchantment in the later years of marriage." Marriage and Family Living 23: 3-11.

POULSHOCK, S. W. and G. T. DEIMLING (1984) "Families caring for elders in residence: issues in the measurement of burden." Gerontologist 39: 230-239.

PUGLISI, J. T. (1983) "Self perceived age changes in sex role concept." International Journal of Aging and Human Development 16: 183-191.

———and D. W. JACKSON (1980-1981) "Sex role identity and self esteem in adulthood." International Journal of Aging and Human Development 12: 129-138.

RILEY, M. W. (1983) "The family in an aging society: a matrix of latent relationships." Journal of Family Issues 4: 439-454.

ROBERTS, W. L. (1979-1980) "Significant elements in the relationship of long-married couples." International Journal of Aging and Human Development 10: 265-272.

ROBERTSON, J. F. (1977) "Grandmotherhood: a study of role conceptions." Journal of Marriage and the Family 39: 165-174.

———(1976) "Significance of grandparents: perceptions of young adult grandchildren." Gerontologist 16: 137-140.

———(1975) "Interaction in three generation families, parents as mediators: toward a theoretical perspective." International Journal of Aging and Human Development 6: 103-110.

ROBINSON, P. (1983) "The sociological perspective," in R. B. Weg (ed.) Sexuality in Later Life. New York: Academic.

ROLLINS, B. C. and K. L. CANNON (1974) "Marital satisfaction over the family life cycle: a reevaluation." Journal of Marriage and the Family 36: 271-282.

ROSE, C. and B. BELL (1971) Predicting Longevity. Lexington, MA: D. C. Heath.

ROSS, H. G. and J. I. MILGRAM (1982) "Important variables in adult sibling relationships: a qualitative study," in M. E. Lamb and B. Sutton-Smith (eds.) Sibling Relationships: Their Nature and Significance Across the Lifespan. Hillsdale, NJ: Lawrence Erlbaum.

SANDERS, L. T. and W. C. SEELBACH (1981) "Variations in preferred care alternatives for the elderly: family versus nonfamily sources." Family Relations 30: 447-451.

SCHLESINGER, M., S. TOBIN, and R. KULYS (1980) "The responsible child and parental well-being." Journal of Gerontological Social Work 3: 3-16.

SCHORR, A. L. (1960) Filial Responsibility in the Modern American Family. Washington, DC: Government Printing Office.

SCHRAM, R. W. (1979) "Marital satisfaction over the family life cycle: a critique and proposal." Journal of Marriage and the Family 411: 7-12.

SCOTT, J. P. (1983) "Siblings and other kin," in T. H. Brubaker (ed.) Family Relationships in Later Life. Beverly Hills, CA: Sage.

————and V. R. KIVETT (1980) "The widowed, black, older adult in the rural South: implications for policy." Family Relations 29: 83-90.

SEELBACH, W. C. (1978) "Correlates of aged parents' filial responsibility expectations and realizations." Family Coordinator 27: 341-350.

————and C. J. HANSEN (1980) "Satisfaction with family relations among the elderly." Family Relations 29: 91-96.

————and W. J. SAUER (1977) "Filial responsibility expectations and morale among aged parents." Gerontologist 17: 492-499.

SHANAS, E. (1980) "Older people and their families: the new pioneers." Journal of Marriage and the Family 42: 9-15.

————(1979a) "The family as a social support system in old age." Gerontologist 19: 169-174.

————(1979b) "Social myth as hypothesis: the case of the family relations of old people." Gerontologist 19: 3-9.

SILVERSTONE, B. and H. K. HYMAN (1982) You and Your Aging Parent. New York: Pantheon.

SINGH, B. and J. WILLIAMS (1981) "Childlessness and family satisfaction." Research on Aging 3: 218-227.

SINNOTT, J. D. (1982) "Correlates of sex roles of older adults." Journal of Gerontology 37: 587-594.

————(1977) "Sex role consistency, biology and successful aging." Gerontologist 17: 459-463.

SMART, M. S. and R. C. SMART (1975) "Recalled, present, and predicted satisfaction in stages of the family life cycle in New Zealand." Journal of Marriage and the Family 37: 408-415.

SPANIER, G. B., R. A. LEWIS, and C. L. COLE (1975) "Marital adjustment over the family life cycle: the issue of curvilinearity." Journal of Marriage and the Family 37: 264-275.

SPASOFF, R. A., A. S. KRAUS, E. J. BEATTIE, D. HOLDEN, J. S. LAWTON, M. RODENBURG, and G. W. WOODCOCK (1978) "A longitudinal study of elderly residents of long-stay institutions." Gerontologist 18: 281-292.

SPORAKOWSKI, M. J. and G. HUGHSTON (1978) "Prescriptions for happy marriage: adjustments and satisfactions of couples married for 50 or more years." Family Coordinator 27: 321-327.

SPRINGER, D. and T. H. BRUBAKER (1984) Family Caregivers and Dependent Elderly. Beverly Hills, CA: Sage.

STINNETT, N., J. COLLINS, and J. E. MONTGOMERY (1972) "Marital need satisfaction of older husbands and wives." Journal of Marriage and the Family 32: 428-434.

STOLLER, E. P. (1983) "Parental caregiving by adult children." Journal of Marriage and the Family 45: 851-858.

STREIB, G. F. and R. W. BECK (1980) "Older families: a decade review." Journal of Marriage and the Family 42: 937-956.

SUSSMAN, M. B. (1977) "Family, bureaucracy, and the elderly individual: an organizational/linkage perspective," in E. Shanas and M. B. Sussman (eds.) Family, Bureaucracy, and the Elderly. Durham, NC: Duke University Press.

————(1976) "Family life of old people," in R. H. Binstock and E. Shanas (eds.) Handbook of Aging and Social Sciences. New York: Van Nostrand Reinhold.

SZINOVACZ, M. (1980) "Female retirement: effects on spousal roles and marital adjustment." Journal of Family Issues 1: 423-440.

TIMBERLAKE, E. M. (1980) "The value of grandchildren to grandmothers." Journal of Gerontological Social Work 3: 63-76.

TREAS, J. (1981) "The great American fertility debate: generational balance and support of the aged." Gerontologist 21: 98-103.

————(1977) "Family support for the aged: some social and demographic considerations." Gerontologist 17: 486-491.

————and A. VANHILST (1976) "Marriage and remarriage rates among older Americans." Gerontologist 16: 132-136.

TROLL, L. E. (1983) "Grandparents: the family watchdogs," in T. H. Brubaker (ed.) Family Relationships in Later Life. Beverly Hills, CA: Sage.

————(1980) "Grandparenting," in L. W. Poon (ed.) Aging in the 1980s: Psychological Issues. Washington, DC: American Psychological Association.

————S. J. MILLER, and R. C. ATCHLEY (1979) Families in Later Life. Belmont: CA: Wadsworth.

UHLENBERG, P. and M. A. MYERS (1981) "Divorce and the elderly." Gerontologist 21: 276-282.

U. S. Department of Health and Human Services (1984) "Advance report of final divorce statistics, 1981." Monthly Vital Statistics Report 32.

U. S. Department of Commerce (1983) "Marital status and living arrangements: March, 1982," in U. S. Bureau of the Census, Current Population Reports, Series P-20, No. 380. Washington, DC: Government Printing Office.

VERWOERDT, A., E. PFEIFFER, and H. WANG (1970) "Sexual behavior in senescence," in E. Palmore (ed.) Normal Aging, Vol. 1. Durham, NC: Duke University Press.

VINICK, B. H. (1978) "Remarriage in old age." Family Coordinator 27: 359-363.

WALKER, A. J. and L. THOMPSON (1983) "Intimacy and intergenerational aid and contact among mothers and daughters." Journal of Marriage and the Family 45: 841-849.

WARD, R. A. (1979) "The never-married in later life." Journal of Gerontology 34: 861-869.

WEEKS, J. R. and J. B. CUELLAR (1981) "The role of family members in the helping networks of older people." Gerontologist 21: 388-394.

WILSON, K. B. and M. R. DeSHANE (1982) "The legal rights of grandparents: a preliminary discussion." Gerontologist 22: 67-71.

WOEHRER, C. E. (1978) "Cultural pluralism in American families: the influence of ethnicity on social aspects of aging." Family Coordinator 27: 329-340.

WOLF, J. H., N. BRESLAU, A. B. FORD, H. D. ZIEGLER, and A. WARD (1983) "Distance and contacts: interactions of black urban elderly adults with their children." Journal of Gerontology 38: 465-471.

WOOD, V. and J. F. ROBERTSON (1976) "The significance of grandparenthood," in J. F. Gubrium (ed.) Time, Roles, and Self in Old Age. New York: Human Sciences.

YARROW, M. R., P. BLANK, O. W. QUINN, E. G. YOUMANS, and J. STEIN (1971) Human Aging. Washington, DC: Government Printing Office.

YORK, J. L. and R. J. CASLYN (1977) "Family involvement in nursing homes." Gerontologist 17: 500-505.

Index

140 LATER LIFE FAMILIES

Deljavan, F., 33
Denigola, P., 37
Dentler, R. A., 29
DeShane, M. R., 77
Deutscher, I., 29
Dissynchronized retirement: See Retirement marriages
Divorced elderly: and family network, 122-123; and grandparents, 76-77, 78; characteristics of, 111-112; golden wedding couples, 40; number of, 18, 20-21, 106, 107, 109; separation, 109-111; types of, 107-109; versus widowed, 112-113
Dobson, C., 34, 35
Dowd, J. J., 53
Dressel, P. L., 24, 36, 39, 42, 43
Duvall, E. M., 13, 14, 15, 16

Ellithorpe, E., 56
Empty nest, 15, 16, 17
Extended family, 83

Family and/or marital history, 17-18, 28, 33, 40, 45, 57, 60, 70
Family life cycle: definition, 13; stages of, 13, 14-16
Family of orientation, 13, 14
Femininity: See Sex roles
Fengler, A. P., 32, 33, 45
Fictive kin, 84, 85, 114, 116
Filial responsibility: feeling of obligation, 51-52; filial maturity, 51-52; racial differences, 52
Fisher, L. R., 72, 73, 77
Ford, A. B., 53
Foster, D., 42
Fox, J., 42

Garza, J. M., 36, 39
Gebhard, P. H., 37
Gender differentiation: in household tasks, 33-35; in personality, 35-36
Generations: and exchange patterns, 54-57; and frequency of contact, 52-54; and households, 57-60; complexity of, 65; future of, 55-66; implications of, 51; size and number of, 50-51, 65
Generational exchanges: all various minority groups, 55; and divorced, 56;

and employment status, 55-56; and life satisfaction, 56; and widowhood, 94-99; black families, 54-55; patterns of, 54-57; types of assistance, 54-57
Gianturco, D. T., 22
Glenn, N. D., 29
Glick, P. C., 16, 22, 40, 107, 109
Golden wedding couples: as survivors, 40; continuity, 41; household tasks, 35, 41; marital quality of, 40, 41; number of, 40
Goodrich, N., 45
Grandparenthood: age differences in, 70; and divorce, 76-77; and research needs, 77-79; as family watchdogs, 71; becoming a grandparent, 72-73; grandchildren's view of, 75-76; meanings of, 71-72; types of, 73-74; value of, 71
Greene, V. L., 62
Grief or grieving process, 91-93, 95
Gubrium, J. F., 30, 115
Gutmann, D. L. 35

Hacker, A., 22
Hagestad, G. O., 66, 107, 111
Hanson, S. L., 52, 53
Harel, Z., 62
Harris, L., 100
Hartshorne, T. S., 75
Hays, J. A., 53
Heineman, G. D., 96
Hennon, C. B., 32, 34, 61, 107, 112
Henrette, J. C., 31
Hess, B., 51, 83
Herr, J. J., 84
Heyman, D. K., 32
Hicks, M. W., 28, 29
Hill, R. B., 53
Hoffman, E., 75
Holahan, C. K., 35
Holden, D., 61
Hook, W. F., 61
Household tasks: after retirement, 33-34; and widowerhood, 99-100; continuation of, 35; division of responsibility, 33-35; traditional patterns, 33-35; within dual-earner marriages, 34; within dual-retired marriages, 34; within golden anniversary marriages, 35, 41

About the Author

Timothy H. Brubaker is a Professor in the Department of Home Economics and Consumer Sciences and an Associate of the Family and Child Studies Center, Miami University, Oxford, Ohio. He has edited a book entitled *Family Relationships in Later Life* (Sage Publications, 1983) and has co-authored another, *Family Caregivers and Dependent Elderly: Minimizing Stress and Maximizing Independence* (Sage Publications, 1984). His research has been published in numerous scholarly journals and focuses on the division of household responsibility, long-term relationships, and service delivery to the elderly and their families.